60p

The Royal Bank
of Scotland

Successful
Expansion for
Small
Businesses

Danny Moss and
Laurence Clarke

First published 1990
by Charles Letts & Co Ltd
Diary House, Borough Road, London SE1 1DW

© Laurence Clarke and Danny Moss

Illustrations: Kevin Jones Associates
© Charles Letts & Co Ltd

British Library Cataloguing in Publication Data
Clarke, Laurence
    Successful expansion for small businesses
    1. Great Britain. Small firms. Expansion. Management
    I. Title   II. Moss, Danny
    658' .022' 0941

ISBN 0-85097-882-3

Readers please note: Some of the information in this book, particularly that which is
directly influenced by government policy, and the contact addresses and telephone
numbers of useful organizations, is liable to change. From May 1990 the London
telephone code *01* will be replaced by *071* or *081*.
    It should also be noted that, where words have been used which denote the masculine
gender only, they shall be deemed to include the feminine gender, and vice versa.

)4566 120164 7 10

Printed and bound in Great Britain by
Charles Letts (Scotland) Ltd

Foreword

Expansion – the welcome headache

The problems facing an expanding business are sometimes no easier than those confronting a struggling business. They are always, however, more welcome both to a company and to its bankers.

It is worth stressing that the way in which a firm tackles expansion is no less important than the way in which it prepares for start-up.

We have a wealth of expertise built up from dealing with other firms' growing pains. I hope that this book, designed to help small businesses become big businesses, will encourage you to take advantage of that experience.

Bob Maiden
Managing Director
The Royal Bank of Scotland

The Authors

Laurence Clarke BSc (Hons), MBA, MCIM, MBZM

After graduating with joint honours in mathematics and astronomy from Glasgow, Laurence Clarke gained a teaching qualification and spent two years in education research before joining the Scottish National Orchestra as Marketing Officer. His MBA from Strathclyde prompted a move into small business development when he set up and was the first General Manager of a Warber Co-op bakery. He then moved on to be Chief Executive of an advertising agency for six years before joining the Scottish Enterprise Foundation to lecture in small business marketing and growth. Laurence Clarke has helped numerous small businesses grow into larger ones and is now further in his own consultancy covering growth and training in The Taylor Clarke Partnership.

Danny Moss BA (Hons), MA MCIM, MIPR: Director of Public Relations programmes, University of Stirling

After graduating with a first class honours degree in business studies from Leeds, Danny Moss worked in marketing and advertising for some seven years. In 1983, he moved into the academic world to lecture in marketing and business at Manchester Polytechnic and UMIST. During this time he also headed the Small Business Unit at Manchester Polytechnic. In 1984 he joined the Scottish Enterprise Foundation at the University of Stirling working on programmes to help small and medium sized businesses in Scotland. Danny Moss has now moved back into the area of marketing and public relations and is currently the director of Public Relations programmes at the University of Stirling.

Contents

Introduction

Think about your small business

What do you want it to be like in five years' time?

Since you are reading this book the answer must be: bigger, better and more successful. But by how much? And, as the owner-manager, where will you fit in? What will you be doing? What do you *want* to be doing? If you do not know where you are going, then this book obviously cannot help you get anywhere. So take a few minutes to jot down some thoughts, dreams even, as to what you would like your business to be like in five years' time. Successful people all seem to have a very clear idea of where they are going, if you can get a clear picture of where you are going, then all the ways of expanding your business that will be looked at in this book will help you get there.

Most successful businesses have, at one stage or another, formulated and pursued something which can be called a 'mission statement'. Your mission statement is really just a picture of your hopes for the future of your small business put into words. The simpler you make your mission statement, the more it will motivate you and your staff to achieve it. Without this motivation, all the tactics in the world will not get you to where you want to be. So, try to gather together your thoughts into a mission statement that will embrace the ideas and main points of this book, but that will also take into account more individual considerations:

1 Does your business have the potential to expand?
2 What are your opportunities for expansion?
3 What will be the affect on your business of expansion in terms of finances, staffing, relationships, and so on?
4 What are the potential benefits and risks of your different expansion opportunities and how best can they be assessed?
5 What are the main barriers to your expansion and how can they be overcome?
6 How should you plan your expansion?
7 What are the main problems of managing and controlling the expansion of your business?

There is no 'right' way of expanding your business: much of it is through trial and error. However, by approaching the subject of the growth of your business in the systematic way suggested in this book, and taking into account the various points made about each method of expansion, you will be able to reduce the risk, avoid some of the pitfalls and have a much better chance of achieving your mission successfully.

As you read the book you will find ways of expanding your business that suit your situation and others that do not. You should also use your experience to enhance the tactics outlined or modify them. You should ask yourself:

1 How can I make this fit my situation?

2 Does this tend to confirm what I already know or have experienced?

3 What modifications do I need to make to take advantage of a particular tactic?

4 Have I tackled a situation, described in this book, in a different way? What can I learn from that experience?

5 However unique or special my own situation, how can I adapt the information in this book to benefit me?

As you go through the book, you should be building up a strategy of how you are going to achieve your mission statement. This is your strategic plan. You should always have a pen with you when reading the book to jot down ideas as they come to you. Use the margins or have a notebook handy. Gradually you will begin to see your strategic plan emerge. Then, once you have read this book, you should be able to:

a assess whether your business has any potential for expansion

b construct a list of the key questions that you will need to answer before proceeding further

c assess the resources you will need for each of the various methods of expansion

d develop a strategic plan for your business expansion

e draw up a business plan to assist with the raising of any necessary finance required to implement your chosen route for expansion

f gain a lot more satisfaction from running your business

Action

1 Write a mission statement for your business.
2 Give yourself a timescale to achieve it or a timescale to achieve important milestones along the way.

1 Why expand your business?

Aims of this chapter

- To give you an insight into why changes in your business environment, your competitors' strategies and your customers' needs, lead to expansion as the best strategy for your business

- To point out some of the pitfalls of expansion for smaller businesses and to help you to plan to avoid them

- To make you think about the implications of expanding your business for both yourself and your employees

The importance of expansion

No matter what the size of your business, you will always be faced with the challenge of planning for the future. You must continually adapt to the changing environment in which you operate and to the changing nature of the competition you face. Hence the aim of virtually all businesses must be to grow and become more profitable. It is changes in your business and in the wider environment that are the principal reasons for growth. You must, therefore, continually monitor and interpret these changes in terms of their implications for the future prospects for your business. These changes may include:

a your customer base
b products and services demanded by your customers
c the numbers, type and sources of your competitors
d the economic climate affecting the market
e legislation affecting how businesses operate

If you fail to recognize and respond to the opportunities and threats that such changes present, you may find that your very survival is endangered. Successful expansion provides you with the additional resources and power either to take advantage of new opportunities or to fight off new threats.

The following example illustrates the type of dilemma often faced by the small business:

The growth of incomes in the UK in recent years has seen a rapid expansion in the number of people able and willing to eat out in restaurants. This has led to the continued expansion of new restaurants, which have traditionally been a very popular form of business for the small businessman. The owners of a small business which during the 1980s had been successfully operating two restaurants in a medium-sized northern town, had been content to enjoy the rewards of the increased trade without considering further expansion. In 1987 they rejected an opportunity to acquire an additional restaurant business offered for sale in the town, only to find that it was acquired by a major pizza restaurant chain. As a result, they were faced with severe competition and found that their trade was badly affected by the opening of this well-known and heavily promoted new restaurant.

This shows that the small businessman cannot afford to become complacent. Not only must you assess expansion opportunities from the point of view of their attractiveness to your business, you also have to consider the likely threat from new competition taking up the opportunity. This view is reinforced in another example:

A successful high quality greengrocery business, which had established a good regular trade over the years, was approached in 1987 by a local farmers' cooperative wishing to find an outlet for its organically grown produce. The owners refused to stock the produce, believing that there was insufficient demand for the goods given their much higher price. Within a few months however, organically grown fruits, grains and vegetables were successfully offered for sale by several of the major supermarket chains. Soon, a number of the business's regular customers switched to buying their greengrocery at the supermarket because of this factor.

This shows that you have to be constantly aware of changing tastes and trends that can affect your business. Opportunities for expansion can be created by such changes in taste and failing to adapt to them can prove damaging to your existing trade.

Problems associated with expansion

Although expansion has been presented as a positive and often necessary move for most businesses, there are a number of potential drawbacks and problems that have to be faced. When considering expansion you must be aware of the number of key issues or questions that have to be addressed in making the decision of whether and how to expand.

The problem of cash flow

The biggest problem when expanding your business is the havoc played with your cash flow and profits in the short term. Although large businesses can afford negative cash flow and losses for quite a considerable time before seeing the benefits, small businesses cannot. Therefore, you will have to assess the cash flow and profitability implications of any opportunity you wish to pursue. This will be discussed more fully in Chapter 11. However, two points are worth noting:

1 Do not be optimistic. Assess your potential cash flow on three levels: very pessimistic, quite pessimistic and what you actually believe.
2 Enter your data onto a computer. It can then be altered to chart the effect of changes of strategy and/or circumstances.

Selecting the particular opportunity to pursue will depend heavily on the results of your cash flow projection and your estimates of the likely trading profit/loss it will incur over, say, two years.

This highlights the first major question that any business must answer when considering expansion: what is the expected payback period on investment in the type of business being considered, and can this be financed out of existing resources or from borrowings?

The need for information

A second problem commonly faced by small businesses considering expansion is their lack of detailed and accurate information about the marketplace and the factors likely to affect it. Small businesses often have particular problems in forecasting the future sales potential of the markets in which they are interested. As a result, decisions often have to be taken with a high degree of uncertainty. This can have two different effects. On the one hand, it can influence you to choose more conservative and shorter term expansion opportunities in order to reduce the degree of uncertainty and risk as far as possible. On the other hand, it can lead you to make a rash and ill-judged move into a business based on what may amount to little more than guesswork and surmise about its future prospects.

An example of the problems that can result from decisions based on inadequate information is illustrated in the following case:

A manufacturer of outdoor light fittings for households, which were sold via independent electrical retailers and garden centres, was offered the opportunity in 1986 to manufacture and distribute under licence an outdoor security light in the United Kingdom. The company were given samples of the light to evaluate, which their salesmen showed to some of their major customers. The company's two salesmen reported an encouraging response from retailers to the samples shown to them, although no firm orders were taken at the time. The company's owners decided to proceed and invested in additional machinery and recruited additional labour. However, when the actual units became available the expected sales failed to materialize. The owners discovered all too late that although the trade had been impressed with the light they were reluctant to take on any new unproven product lines. In addition, the company discovered that a similar light had recently gone on sale by mail order at a lower price than their own.

Clearly you have to research your markets thoroughly and ensure you have adequate information on which to base expansion decisions. Thus access to reliable and accurate market information and intelligence is perhaps one of the most important resources for any business trying to plan its future.

So, the second key question for businesses considering expansion is: do we have sufficient information about the market and its prospects on which to base our decisions. If not, can the information be obtained at a realistic cost?

You can draw on a variety of sources of information to assist in assessing the attractiveness of alternative expansion opportunities. These sources of information will be examined in more detail in Chapter 2.

The quest for power

Sometimes decisions to expand a business are mistakenly taken by their owners in the personal quest for status or power in their local community. However, this may cloud your judgement and lead to problems for the business, particularly if this places undue strain on your existing resources. The decision to expand and commit resources to new areas of business should be based on sound business criteria and taking full account of the potential impact on your existing business operations. Often the best way of checking the viability of your idea is to seek the impartial opinion of an experienced business adviser, such as an accountant, bank manager, or small business adviser.

Planned versus unplanned expansion

Expansion can sometimes take place in an unplanned manner: your business simply continuing to grow due to increased demand without any objective thought as to the future implications. However, expansion should be a controlled activity in which you are fully aware of the direction in which you are going and the future demands this will make on your business.

A small printing business trading in Manchester during the 1980s found that it was experiencing a rapid growth in the demand for brochures, bill stickers and other promotional materials from local businesses. Jobs were rarely refused despite the fact that the business's rather outdated printing machinery could not fully cope with the volume of work. This resulted in many of the promised delivery times being missed, much to the annoyance of customers, and although work continued to come in, a number of these dissatisfied customers began to look elsewhere for their printing in order to ensure more reliable delivery. The small business therefore began to lose sales and reputation. Had the business's owner taken a more objective view of the situation he might have recognized the need to invest in new machinery, which would have allowed him to take greater advantage of the increasing business opportunities.

Making use of underutilized resources

Some businesses expand to try to make better use of their resources. You may have spare factory or store space or underutilized manufacturing capacity. In this sense expansion is seen as a means of improving efficiency and reducing unit costs. However, before additional capacity is realized, it is crucial that you make a careful assessment of whether it is justified. You will need to examine future product demand and the additional set-up costs. The timing of the expansion of capacity is the critical factor. Make sure the decision to add capacity is not based on merely short-term fluctuations in demand.

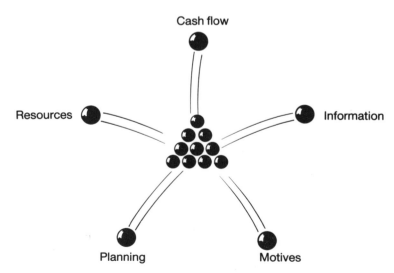

Fig. 1.1 Key areas to be examined when considering expansion

The implications of expansion

The ultimate decision as to whether to try to expand the business and if so by what means lies with you. In many ways this has advantages in that decisions to respond to potential opportunities can be swiftly taken and the necessary developments put in hand without the delays that may be found in a larger, more bureaucratic organization. However, you should ensure your decision is not taken in isolation without seeking out as much advice as possible. Make sure you have a clear picture of:

1 The potential additional demands on your time and that of your employees.
2 The implications for your existing business in terms of the time available to control existing operations and possible effects on existing customers.
3 The additional finance required to put your expansion plan into operation and its effect on the balance sheet and profitability of your existing business.
4 The likely response from competitors to your planned action.
5 All the alternative expansion opportunities. These should be thoroughly worked through to determine their longer term viability and implications for your business. Smaller businesses have relatively limited resources and a decision to expand in one direction will normally preclude others being followed, at least in the short to medium term.

Hence, your aim must be to match your business's resources and strengths to the expansion opportunity which offers the best potential for sustained growth and profits. All these factors should be brought together in a comprehensive business plan, which then can be thoroughly discussed with a professional adviser.

Although expansion, particularly into a new business area, can be something of a step into the unknown, if it is carefully managed it should not present any serious obstacles to the continued success of your business. The watchwords must be **careful evaluation** and **planning based on sound information**.

The subsequent chapters of this book will examine the principal methods of expansion and highlight some of the most important factors that must be considered in selecting any particular one of them. It will also examine the essential steps in managing and controlling the expansion of the business and the main pitfalls that should be avoided.

Action

1 Consider all the options, not just one.
2 Seek the advice of others.
3 Consider the implications of what you intend, for yourself and your employees.
4 Standing still is going backwards so get organized and get started!

2 The obstacles to expansion

Aims of this chapter

- To help you recognize the importance of planning for expansion
- To encourage you to look for obstacles to expansion within your existing business that you can do something about
- To help you assess the likely external obstacles to expansion and begin to devise ways round these

The importance of planning

If, as has been suggested, expansion is almost inevitable for most healthy businesses, why is it that some businesses fail to grow?

The reasons can be attributed to a number of different factors. In some cases, it may be due to the particular circumstances facing the business or to the underlying nature of the industry in which they operate. For example, the building industry is notorious for the cyclical nature of the trade, which can involve prolonged periods of depression in demand, which may in turn handicap any attempts to expand businesses operating in this industry.

However, although fluctuating cycles in trade may affect expansion in the short term, this does not explain why in the longer term businesses fail to expand. The answer is that many businesses fail to anticipate and **plan** for such inevitable downturns in trade and, as a result, they may be severely affected by them, damaging their longer-term growth prospects or even threatening their survival.

Planning is essential in order to understand all the implications of the proposed method of expansion. For example, without a plan, it may be impossible to raise the finance needed to exploit the intended opportunity. Plans will also force you to test your assumptions about the future potential of the market and to question the basis on which you will compete. The aim of planning should be to highlight the principal obstacles to expansion and to identify alternative ways around them. These can then be examined to check their feasibility and the implications for your business.

The obstacles to expansion

Your own attitude

The prospect of periodic downturns in trade that can result from expanding a business may make you reticent to commit yourself to expansion. In effect, this creates a psychological obstacle against the idea of expansion. Most business owners probably see their first priority as to survive. Hence, expansion, with all the risks it involves, may not be an attractive option, particularly in an industry where cycles in trade are the norm.

Therefore, one of the most significant obstacles to expansion is your attitude to risk-taking and your own commitment to expanding the business. Without the necessary commitment, you will find it impossible to get even minimal expansion plans off the ground. If, however, you are committed and become better informed about your markets and understand the cyclical nature of your business, then you will be better prepared for fluctuations in trade and so less likely to be deterred from considering genuine longer-term expansion opportunities. In fact, expansion, especially when it involves diversifying into other business areas, is often the most effective way of countering the fluctuations in trade that can occur within your primary area of business.

A small builder, who specialized in the construction of medium priced houses and flats, saw his business grow steadily during the late 1970s, and early 1980s. However, the builder, aware of the cyclical nature of the industry, began to expand the property maintenance side of his business and was thus better placed to withstand the downturn in demand that severely affected the construction industry in general during the mid-1980s. This expansion of his operations also placed him in a strong position to capitalize on the next major upturn in the building trade during the late 1980s.

 So, your commitment to expansion and your willingness to accept some degree of risk, are critical to the success of the expansion of your business.

More tangible internal and external obstacles

These include:

1 Access to the necessary finance.
2 Access to other resources.
3 Access to necessary skilled labour and management.
4 Access to the necessary market channels.
5 Competitor activities that block expansion plans.

Form of obstacle	Externally originating	Internally originating
Access to finance	Generally the problem is to persuade external institutions to loan funds	Poor financial management may exacerbate the problem. Internally generated funding may be the cheapest source of new capital
Access to other resources	Generally the problem is to identify sources of the necessary resources and to negotiate acceptable terms for supply	Poor resource management can cause problems and handicap expansion plans
Access to skilled labour and management	Generally the problem stems from the inability of the small business to compete in the labour market in terms of pay and conditions	Lack of attention to training and staff development can cause shortages of skilled labour
Access to market channels	Large competitors can 'swamp' the market and have the twin advantages of immense bargaining power and of centralized buying	Failure to make product 'different' from competitors' and lack of interest in alternative methods of selling
Competitors' blocking activities	Competitors may take action to raise barriers to entry or restrict expansion in the existing market	Failure to monitor competitors activity and to signal intentions may provoke unexpected responses
Local government interference	Planning permission and licensing legislation can be a barrier	Failure to keep up to date on current legislation or to liaise with local planning officers may exacerbate the problems
Industry or market conditions	Changes in the nature of demand or in the nature of competition can present obstacles. Entry into new markets may depend on the strength of the existing competition	—
Technology	Costs of the necessary technology may be prohibitive. The rate of change in technology may be a deterrent to expansion	The failure to monitor changes in technology and to invest in new technology can handicap expansion

Fig. 2.1 A classification of obstacles to expansion

6 Local government legislation that prevents you from pursuing a chosen form of expansion.
7 The actual nature of the market or industry in which you operate.
8 Technological barriers to expansion.

These obstacles can originate both from external sources and from within your business. However, most businesses tend to concentrate on the external barriers to expansion, neglecting or becoming unaware of the obstacles presented by the internal failings of the business. For example, your attitude to risk-taking has already been shown as a potentially significant obstacle; and the problems presented by a shortage of skilled labour may be due, at least partially, to a failure by the business to invest in the training of its workforce. It is important, therefore, for the business to recognize the potential sources of obstacles to expansion, and understand which of them it has a greater ability to influence or control.

It is possible to classify obstacles to expansion according to their internal or external origin. This may help you to recognize the extent to which you can directly act to overcome them. A classification of the more commonly encountered obstacles to expansion is shown in fig. 2.1 on the previous page.

1 **Access to finance.** Perhaps the most commonly cited obstacle to expansion is the problem of raising the necessary finance to fund the expansion plans. Many business people complain that banks and other potential lending institutions are reluctant to lend money to smaller businesses, particularly those that do not have an established track record with the potential lender. Whilst there is undoubtedly an element of truth in this assertion, the growth of the 'enterprise movement' in the UK in recent years, has witnessed a dramatic change in attitudes of banks in particular, to lending to smaller businesses. There has also been a growth of other lending institutions prepared to back sound business ideas, most notably the venture capital companies such as 3i (Investors in Industry), as well as the local development sections of large companies such as British Coal and British Steel. The latter two are specialist subsidiaries of their parent companies, established to help revive the local economy in areas where the parent company has traditionally been the main employer, through support for new and existing businesses.

Advice on sources of funding for smaller businesses is normally readily available from Local Enterprise Agencies and specialist small business advisers. The address of your nearest Local Enterprise Agency can be obtained from:

Business in the Community, 227a City Rd, London EC1 4GH. Tel: 01 253 3716.

The Department of Trade and Industry (DTI) can give further and detailed advice on sources of funding. Some parts of the country are designated Development or Assisted Areas and the Department of Employment will give information on the grants that are available for expanding your business if you are located in one of these areas. The British Overseas Trade Board can advise on grants which are available to assist exporters. Some grants are also available from the European Community, contact the DTI for details.

However, it is important to appreciate the necessary steps in preparing an application for funding support for expansion. It is essential that a detailed business plan is prepared. This should cover both the state of the existing business and the prospects for proposed expansion venture, and should seek to show:

a the current nature of your business and its track record
b the nature of the current market(s) served and the future projected trends
c the current and projected cash flow, profit/loss and balance sheets of your business
d the level of experience of yourself and your current management

These details provide the potential lender with a picture of the health of the current business and help generate confidence in the likely success of the projected plans. You should then outline the proposed new venture showing in more detail:

a the nature of the proposed expansion opportunity
b the projected potential of the target market and expected profits and cash flow that would be generated
c the capability of the business to exploit the opportunity
d the necessary investment needed to exploit the opportunity and the amount, if any, that the business will be funding itself
e the amount of money sought and the time period over which the money is required
f what security the business can offer for any loan

A well-prepared expansion plan will give you a reasonable chance of obtaining funding from one or other of the various lending institutions. Without a detailed plan, however, potential lenders will be very reluctant to commit their institution's funds to your expansion plans.

It is also important that the expansion plans are realistically drawn up. It is pointless trying to deceive potential supporters with overoptimistic projections, because even if the funding is obtained, you may find yourself in serious trouble if sales fail to live up to forecasts or costs massively exceed those projected. The expansion plan will also be of great benefit to your own business purposes as the drawing up of the plan will help crystallize your thinking about the proposed expansion opportunity and force you to ask yourself some hard questions about its true viability.

2 Access to other resources. Although funding is usually seen as the most critical resource, access to other resources can be equally important. For, example, you may require additional specialist components or raw materials that are in short supply. It is crucial that you ensure that you can obtain sufficient supplies of such inputs *at realistic costs*. This is particularly important where there are few suppliers of the necessary inputs, and you would not be a major customer for them. In times of shortage or excess demand you could find yourself vulnerable to price rises or even find your supply cut off.

The availability of land or premises can also be critical to your expansion plans. In most cases, local authority planning permission will be needed for new premises or the conversion of existing buildings. The timetable of the planned expansion can be significantly affected by delays in local authority planning procedures, and the possible effects of delays in bringing new facilities on-stream must be taken into account in the planning of any expansion.

3 Access to skilled labour and management. Where the planned expansion involves the production of goods that require particular skills or expertise, the availability of a pool of skilled labour or management expertise can be an important factor. However, you may have to compete with larger companies, requiring the same expertise, for such skilled personnel. Usually, the smaller business cannot afford to match the salaries and benefits offered by larger companies, and you may thus find it difficult to attract or retain particular categories of workers. This will play a very influential part in your expansion plans.

JobCentres are a useful source of information on the availability of skilled workers and they keep a record of the skills of the unemployed people who are on their books.

4 Access to market channels. Many retail markets are now dominated by the larger multiple retail groups, for example food retailing is dominated by the major supermarket groups such as Tesco, Sainsbury, ASDA, Gateway, Safeway, Marks & Spencer and Waitrose. Similarly the 'do-it-yourself' sector is increasingly dominated by the DIY superstores such as B & Q, Texas, Payless, Do-It-All and Homebase. These retail groups obviously have considerable bargaining power in their respective markets, and if you are unable to persuade one or more of them to stock your products, then your chances of success in the respective market may be severely affected. Often smaller businesses encounter the obstacle of centralized buying: the system whereby products are purchased centrally for all of a company's outlets. If you are unable to supply goods in the quantities generally required, then it may not be possible to persuade the particular company to purchase them at all. Equally, small businesses often have to compete with more established and possibly larger competitors to attract the interest of buyers and to persuade them of the merits of their products.

Ultimately, retail buyers will be swayed by what they feel will be the likely demand for the products they stock. The smaller business, unable to afford the heavy advertising support for its products that larger companies can often afford to undertake, obviously has a harder task to convince retail buyers of the potential attraction of its products. However, many retail buyers will normally consider any product that is fundamentally different and likely to appeal to its customers.

If your planned expansion requires access to retail markets, then you must identify the most suitable retail channels and realistically assess which retail outlets are likely to accept your product. One approach that may encourage the stocking of the product is giving exclusive distribution rights to one particular retail group. It may also be necessary to look at alternative methods of selling your goods, such as by mail order or by using sales agents to help gain distribution for your product. Finally, if you are unable to secure adequate distribution for your products, you could, as a last resort, consider a move into retailing yourself. For example, unhappy at the large retail margins that were being put on her handmade jewellery, one Scottish jewellery designer decided to open her own shop in Glasgow which is now trading very successfully. However, do bear in mind that this obviously involves a major expansion of your business.

5 Competitors' blocking activities. The nature and strength of the competition that your business would face if expanding its activities either into new markets or within its existing markets, can be a significant obstacle to expansion.

Existing businesses in a new market are likely to seek to deter any new entrants or to at least prevent them from securing a significant share of the market. Equally, existing competitors are likely to resist attempts to erode their share of the market. The typical competitor activities that you may have to overcome in order to establish yourself in a new market or expand existing market operations include:

1 Price wars to undercut the ruling prices in the market and hence make entry less profitable or prevent the loss of market share.
2 Increased advertising support to maintain brand loyalty and make entry expensive.
3 Exclusive distribution or supply arrangements to prevent new businesses gaining the necessary distribution or supply of essential raw materials.
4 Heavy trade promotions to reduce the shelf space allocated to any new products.

Your ability to overcome such competitor activity will depend very much on your resources and careful forward planning.

However, the severity of your competitors' defensive actions will depend on the seriousness of the threat that they perceive you to pose to them. In many cases you may be able to gain a bridgehead into a new market without undue competitor reaction. Once established in a new market, you will be in a stronger position to resist competitor activity. Similarly expansion in existing markets may have to be undertaken gradually to assess competitor reactions before undertaking a major investment in expansion.

Ultimately, competition must be accepted as a fact of life, but you can at least plan how to cope with the likely competitive reaction. Such plans should take account of the 'worst case scenario' (i.e. the worst that could possibly happen) and how this would affect the business.

6 Local government interference. Expansion plans can be delayed or even blocked by local government legislation or their refusal to grant you planning permission or licences. Often the granting of local government planning permission can be delayed due to technicalities with the planning application procedures, or due to local objections. This can of course prove both frustrating and expensive. It is advisable to use experienced architects and lawyers to handle the more complex planning of licensing applications, and, where possible, the appropriate local authority officials should be approached openly to discuss any likely objections to the plans in advance. This can avoid delays due to small technical problems that could be adjusted in the plans prior to their formal submission. Ultimately if planning permission is refused the business can appeal to central government for the decision to be overturned. However, this can be a lengthy and costly process and for many small businesses may not be worthwhile.

Equally, licences for restaurants, hotels, and so on are granted at local level and it is important if you are seeking to expand in this area, to maintain good relations with the police, fire officers and building inspectors, in order to gain any constructive criticisms of the proposed plans at an early stage. These criticisms can be rectified before the expansion plans are submitted to the appropriate body thereby increasing the chance of the plans being passed first time and saving costly delay.

> The owners of a Chinese restaurant, seeking to expand their business by moving to larger and more prestigious premises, almost went out of business when their drinks licence was blocked by a local councillor. Although it took the owners almost a year, they persevered and eventually won their drinks licence at central government level.

7 The nature of your market or industry. The fact that your market is stagnant or even contracting makes expansion more difficult, competition becomes greater and prices and margins tend to fall. It is possible, however, to take advantage of this situation if you are in a healthy financial position. You can start picking up the customers of those businesses that fail and acquire those firms that are struggling, at a cheap price. Nevertheless, there comes a time when you must move out of that market or face eventual limits to your growth, or even existence.

Your industry may, for example, have restrictions on what you can and can't do. Law firms, for instance, are heavily confined by the Law Society as to the promotional tools they can use and this can present a partial barrier to their growth.

Finally, it may simply be that the competition in your own market is too great for you to contemplate expansion of your existing business.

> John Black of Greenock Sail and Tent recognized that large sailmakers from the South of England had such a hold on the yacht sail making market that any expansion of his business could not be in this area. He decided to concentrate on other uses of canvas as protective coverings for industry where there were few if any competitors.

8 Technological obstacles. Although perhaps not as common a problem for smaller businesses as the other factors discussed, technology can in various ways pose a barrier to expansion. Firstly, the particular technology used in an industry by its more competitive firms may require a high level of investment. Access to this technology may be beyond your resources and to use older technology may make you uncompetitive. Secondly, where technology is changing rapidly in an industry, it may deter businesses from expanding their current activities for fear that they will become outdated and uncompetitive. Changing technology can also create uncertainty surrounding the future demand for products, which can again be a deterrent to plans to expand the existing business. An example of the impact of changing technology can be seen in the market for micro-computers.

The growth of demand for micro-computers for home and business use has undergone rapid growth and change during the past 10 to 20 years. Many small businesses have, over the years, entered the market as dealers supplying both hardware and software systems. However, the market has seen dramatic changes in computer technology which has forced some manufacturers out of business, whilst at the same time reducing the prices of computers and software. Some of the better known equipment suppliers during the earlier years, such as Acorn, Commodore and Apricot have seen their share of the market cut dramatically, whilst Amstrad and a string of IBM 'clone' machines manufacturers have come to dominate the market. As a result, many dealers have been forced out of business as demand for the machines they stocked fell and new patterns of supply to customers emerged. The specialist dealer has been replaced by the high street retailer such as Dixons.

This example illustrates how changing technology can create opportunities as well as threats to a business. Expansion plans that are centred on markets experiencing marked changes in the technology of the products sold must be viewed cautiously, and overcommitment to one form of technology avoided.

Overcoming the obstacles

Expansion is rarely trouble free, and inevitably you will experience at least some obstacles to your growth, irrespective of whether this is in your existing markets or in new markets. However, most obstacles can be overcome, even though it may involve a radical change to at least some aspects of the initial expansion plan.

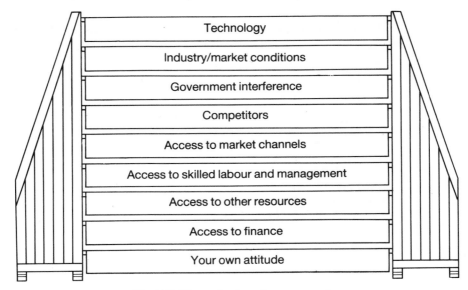

Fig. 2.2 The main obstacles to expansion

The key factor in overcoming obstacles to expansion, is **detailed and thorough planning**.

As a result of examining the actual and potential obstacles, it may be necessary to revise your expansion plans or even defer them. However, this will help you avoid a rash and potentially disastrous move into an area that you are perhaps ill-equipped to exploit, and which could seriously damage the prospects for your existing business operations. Equally, careful planning, involving an examination of potential obstacles, may highlight previously unconsidered opportunities for expansion which may prove more profitable than those you originally considered.

Action

1 Assess how much risk you are willing to take and hence your commitment to any expansion plan.
2 Assess whether you are creating internal obstacles to expansion by:

    a poor financial management
    b poor resource management
    c lack of training and staff development

    d failure to monitor competitor activity
    e failure to keep up to date on current legislation
    f failure to monitor changes in technology and do
      something about them

3 List any potential external obstacles and jot down any ways
  round them that you can think of. You should consider:

    a access to finance
    b access to other resources
    c access to skilled labour
    d access to market channels
    e competitor activity
    f local government powers
    g industry/market conditions
    h changing technology

3 Expansion: the choices available

Aims of this chapter

- To outline the different options available for expanding your business

- To introduce you to the approximate levels of risk, speed of growth, and potential of each of the options

- To emphasize how important it is to know where you are going and to analyse where you currently stand. This will involve a SWOT analysis where the strengths and weaknesses of your company are looked at along with the opportunities and threats that exist in the environment in which you trade

Expansion: the main points

Measuring expansion

Expansion means different things to different people. Solicitors and accountants often measure growth by the number of partners they have, and how often have you heard other owner-managers boast about their increased turnover or the bigger premises they have moved into? Many businesses, particularly cooperatives, see expansion in terms of the number of people they employ. And many entrepreneurs will look at the size of their car or even the number of businesses they have as a measure of expansion.

You will need to decide what 'type' of expansion you are thinking of and how to measure it. This book is primarily concerned with expansion in terms of profits, although this will normally be achieved by expanding your turnover, and you may have to forgo profits in the short term in order to increase them later. However, other measurables can lead on from this. An increase in turnover may well demand more staff, so if your primary aim is to increase your workforce, this strategy should benefit you as well. Equally, the increase in profits should allow you to achieve better premises or cars if you measure expansion in that way.

Methods of expansion

Once you have decided how you are going to measure your business's expansion, there are a number of ways of achieving it:

1 Expansion of existing business. Where the emphasis is on increasing your share of the existing market, using your existing product or service range.

> Tom Farmer of Kwik-Fit started with one garage and gradually expanded his business by opening other garages until he now owns a nationwide multimillion pound operation. He stuck with the product and market that he knew best in order to develop his business.

2 Expansion into new markets. Here the existing range of products or services is maintained but efforts are made to find new markets for them. These markets may be different areas of the UK, different applications of the product or service, or the existing application but different user groups.

> Susan Harvey of Harvey Maps had supplied the orienteering sport for a number of years with maps and equipment, when she decided to find out if she could also supply schools. She set up a mail order catalogue to supply this new market with her existing product range. The catalogue now accounts for well over a third of her business and is increasing every year.

3 Expansion via new products or services. Selling to your existing markets and, more particularly, your existing customers, new products or services that use predominantly your present staff and production facilities.

> Liquid Levers was set up by Nigel and Irene Buchanan after Nigel, who owned a garage, invented a labour-saving machine to bleed brakes. Nigel won an award for his invention and has since developed five other highly innovative products for the garage trade. Liquid Levers appears regularly on *Tomorrow's World* and is growing fast through the use of new products in an existing market.

4 Expansion by diversification. Here the company goes into entirely new businesses or creates new products or services for markets that are entirely new to them.

> Ken Thompson took over his father's construction firm and began to build it up. However he found expansion of the existing business a little slow, so when he found difficulty in obtaining carpeting for some of his contracts he set up a carpet wholesale division which he later expanded into a retail outlet as well.

5 Expansion overseas. Having exhausted most of the potential of the UK market, the company looks to similar markets overseas that will buy the product with as few alterations as possible.

> Former trombonist, Alan Galashan, formed Applied Sweepers and very soon cornered the British market for small road and pavement sweeping machines. His major competitors are two large companies in France. Alan decided that attack was the best form of defence and so he now exports a considerable number of machines to his competitors' home territory. Because his market was saturated at home, Alan Galashan kept his expansion going by venturing overseas.

6 Expansion by takeover or merger. This is a case where expansion is achieved by purchasing, or acquiring an existing company or, more unusually, by joining forces with another company under a single structure formed out of the two.

> David and Jean Clark had owned Findlay Clark's Garden Centre for a number of years when, after trying most other types of growth, they decided to acquire another company. They bid for and acquired Smiths of Hazelhead, an operation at least as big as themselves. Overnight they had expanded their business by over 100 percent. David and Jean found that acquisition was therefore a very quick way to expand.

7 Licensing. Many companies are willing to let you produce their product, or occasionally service, or use their technology, for a fee. This transaction is known as licensing in and can help you minimize your costs. Another method of licensing, called licensing out, is similar to franchising, but without the business expertise that goes with franchising. By this method you can make your successful products or processes generate cash for you by selling them to others and taking a royalty payment on the products or services sold.

8 Expansion by franchising. This is where branches of your business are located all over the country but the ownership of each branch has been sold to someone else. This also includes selling your know-how, technology, or image to others.

> The Body Shop is one of Britain's great success stories. Anita Roddick's speedy rise to fame was made possible by franchising her original idea of a retail outlet selling natural cosmetics and skin care products. She had discovered the staggering speed of expansion that can be achieved through this method.

You can expand your business by looking at franchising from the franchisor's point of view. You can take up an existing franchise and expand your business on a similar fashion to taking over another company or simply expand your operation by franchising a new product or service that is complementary to your existing product or service.

9 Expansion by rationalization. It is often possible to make greater profits by getting rid of the unprofitable aspects of your business, and this in turn may assist in speedier subsequent expansion in terms of turnover and ultimately profits.

Ros Taylor is a clinical psychologist who set up a partnership to provide companies with stress management consultancy. Leimon Taylor, after an initial period of quite quick growth ran into problems and began to lose money. Eventually, Ros was forced to make most of the staff redundant and move to much smaller premises. This move stemmed the losses and she started to make money again. Soon she had a new partner and expanded her business from a now secure base.

This case is a good example of the assertion by the famous American researcher of small business, David Burch, that the best determinant of future success is previous decline.

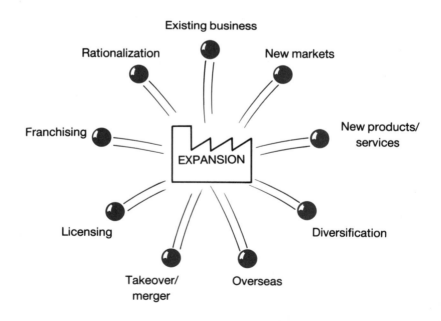

Fig. 3.1 The main methods of expansion

Speed of expansion

Different people look for different rates of expansion. The particular rate you grow at will depend on:

1 The expansion method you have chosen. Fig.3.2 shows what speed of expansion you can expect from each of the ways of expanding your business that have been discussed.

2 Your enthusiasm for expansion. The less committed to growth you are, the slower it will happen. Indeed, expansion is very much a self-fulfilling policy. This is due primarily to the fact that the more enthusiastic you are, the more likely you are to convince others of your plans, and the more likely they are to strive to achieve what you want.

3 The resources of your firm. Clearly, the less money, the less able staff, and the more inappropriate and less efficient equipment and systems you have, the slower your rate of growth.

The risks involved in expansion

Each method of expansion involves a different level of risk. Nevertheless, the *relative* risk levels between the methods of expansion remain much the same. Fig 3.2 shows the general risk levels for each of the ways in which you can expand your small business.

The potential of the different ways of expansion

Certain markets can offer only limited growth due to their size and amount of competitor activity. Equally, some markets may be declining in size, or only growing slowly. Thus not all expansion strategies offer the same long-term potential. Some, like diversification, tackle several markets and hence offer much greater chances of growth. Fig. 3.2 shows the potential of each of the expansion strategies.

The finance required for expansion

This will be examined in a later chapter (see Chapter 11). However, different strategies do require different levels of finance and fig.3.2 illustrates the possible ranges of finance that might be required.

Method of expansion	Speed	Risk	Potential	Amount of finance required
Existing business	Slow	Low	Strictly limited	Small–large
New markets	Moderate	Low	Limited	Small–large
New products or services	Moderate	Medium	Limited	Large
Diversification	Moderate/fast	High	Large	Large
Overseas	Slow	Medium	Reasonable	Small–moderate
Takeover or merger	Fast	High	Unlimited	Small–large
Licensing in	Moderate	Low	Reasonable –large	Moderate
Licensing out	Moderate/fast	Low	Large	Small
Franchising	Fast	Low	Limited– large	Small–large
Rationalization	Moderate	Low	Limited	Small

Fig. 3.2 The different expansion strategies

Mind the gap!

This chapter has examined the various ways of expanding your business and some of the factors that have to be borne in mind. However, this all presupposes that you know where you are going. One of the fundamental mistakes that owner-managers make when considering expansion is to fail to decide where they are going. If you don't know what you are aiming at, how can you possibly decide what strategy to use? Therefore the first rule of small business expansion is:

Decide what you want to achieve by expanding your business

Having decided where you want to be, the next move is to work out where you are. This will involve looking at what is happening outside the business as well as analysing what is going on within the business. A simple way of looking at this is to carry out what is known as a SWOT analysis. This entails looking at:

Strengths – what your company is good at or has going for it.
Weaknesses – what your company is weak at or is deficient in.
Opportunities – when you look outside the firm, what opportunities exist for increased trade.
Threats – again when you look outside the firm, what possible dangers do you see.

Fig. 3.3. shows the gap that exists between where you are and where you want to be. You can bridge that gap with one or more of the strategies that will be discussed in the forthcoming chapters. It is your personal aspirations that drive you across that gap. As the illustration shows, the better you know your present situation and what is happening around you, the sharper and clearer your aspirations become and so the faster and more efficiently you cross the gap. Thus the second rule of expansion is:

● Do a SWOT analysis before you start planning your expansion

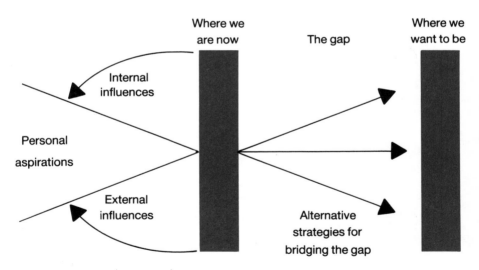

Fig. 3.3 Knowing where you want to go

Action

1 Decide what level of risk you are willing to take and hence which options for growth are open to you.
2 Decide what speed of growth you want and hence what options will provide the rate of expansion you want.

3 Decide whether you have limited or unlimited horizons as to the development of your business.
4 Decide what level of finance you can afford to invest in the project and hence what options are open to you.
5 Carry out a SWOT analysis of your firm and environment, it doesn't need to be too detailed at this stage, but get the strengths, weaknesses, opportunities and threats written down.

4 Planning for expansion

Aims of this chapter

- To examine why planning is important
- To give you an uncomplicated process for planning
- To give you an understanding of the business plan and how to produce it
- To help you monitor and review the importance of communications for expansion

The importance of planning

Although some businesses can and do successfully expand in a more or less haphazard way, they invariably run into problems later when their markets are less buoyant, because they have not learnt the skills of planning. Many businesses can grow and be extremely successful in less than helpful environments, if they just have a carefully thought out strategy.

Nowadays, if you are looking for sources of finance, the banks and lending organizations insist on seeing a business plan before entering into negotiations. The mistake that many people make is to view drawing up a plan as simply something which has to be done in order to get hold of the money, and not as the basis of a programme to guide their business through uncharted waters. By planning your expansion you will be able to assess the viability of any options you are considering and the problems associated with them before starting your expansion.

However, beware of the plan which is based on wishful thinking and that makes unrealistic demands on your resources, capabilities and staff. Always check your plan with your accountant and bank manager, and listen to what they say about it.

Starting planning

When you are planning your expansion you should go through four stages:

1 Analyse your situation.

2 Choose a strategy.
3 Make your strategy happen.
4 Monitor and review your plan.

Analyse your situation

The previous chapter covered the need to carry out a SWOT
analysis for your organization. This is the basis of analysing your
situation. Do make sure that you have looked not only at your
competitors and market but also the environment in which you
operate. Environmental factors you should consider include:

The economy:	For example, what will happen to interest rates?
Social and cultural changes:	For example, how will the drop in the numbers of school leavers affect you?
Technological changes:	For example, are there changes in the way your products are made, or services delivered that are already happening elsewhere or in the pipeline that could make your processes inefficient or obsolete?
Political changes:	For example, what new government policies are being considered that would affect the way you operate your business?

In practice all four of these factors may be interrelated, with
changes in any one having a 'knock-on' effect on others. For
example, changes in technology may have significant effects on the
operating costs of industry and hence on the economics of the
business, or in some cases may have some potentially harmful side
effects that cause governments to introduce controls on the ways in
which the new technology is utilized. The growth in recent years of
public sensitivity to environmental or 'green' issues has led to
increased pressure from the public for tighter government control
on waste emissions and pollution. Government has responded by
imposing more restrictive controls on the ways in which many
industries operate. Similarly this concern over the environment has
encouraged many manufacturers to develop less environmentally
harmful products and to invest in new technologies that are less
harmful to the environment. The increased demand for lead-free
petrol is a typical example of this trend.

The SWOT analysis also covers what is happening inside your business. Try to see your strengths and weaknesses in terms of your standing against your competitors. You may also want to rate (see fig. 4.1) how you stand against them by listing a number of attributes and seeing how you and your competitors rate for each on a scale of 1 to 5 (5 being the strongest score).

	You	Competitor 1	Competitor 2	Competitor 3
Machinery	3	5	1	3
Production staff	3	5	3	2
Financial base	2	4	5	1
Sales staff	5	2	3	3
Location	1	2	5	4

Fig. 4.1 Example of a completed chart showing how you might stand against your competitors

Once you have analysed and defined your strengths, weaknesses, opportuntities and threats it is important to rank them in each category. Therefore, to carry out a SWOT analysis in detail, you should also tackle the following:

1 For each category, the six to eight most important factors for the business should be identified (in practice any more than eight factors will tend to lead you to include unimportant or trivial points).
2 These should then be ranked in order of seriousness or importance to your business.
3 The strengths or weaknesses should then, where appropriate, be matched against the identified opportunities or threats.
4 This should lead you to identify a number of priority issues in terms of either significant opportunities that your business has the required strengths to exploit or key threats to which your business is particularly vulnerable.

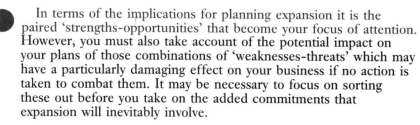

In terms of the implications for planning expansion it is the paired 'strengths-opportunities' that become your focus of attention. However, you must also take account of the potential impact on your plans of those combinations of 'weaknesses-threats' which may have a particularly damaging effect on your business if no action is taken to combat them. It may be necessary to focus on sorting these out before you take on the added commitments that expansion will inevitably involve.

The last stage of analysing your situation is to summarize the key 'strengths-opportunities' that you can realistically consider pursuing.

Choosing a strategy

For each of these key 'strengths-opportunities' you then need to look at the various tactics for expansion reviewed in Chapter 3 and analysed in depth in Chapters 5 to 10. Taking each key 'strength-opportunity' and its associated possible tactics in turn you should assess what would be involved in pursuing each option in terms of:

a the likely financial investment required
b what resources would need to be committed, for example, staff, plant capacity, sales force time, your time
c the likely impact on your existing business operation
d the promotional costs
e any new distribution and sales channels required

These should be balanced against your forecasts of the likely returns from pursuing the option in terms of profit. You may want to calculate how long it will take you to pay back your investment in the option. For instance, say the option involves you buying a new machine but needing no extra staff. If the machine costs £20,000 and you estimate that the sales will be £15,000 per year, then it will take you four years to pay back the investment if your gross margin (sales minus direct costs) is 33 per cent of sales.

$$\text{Pay back period in years} \quad = \quad \frac{\text{Investment in } \pounds \text{s}}{\text{Projected annual gross margin in } \pounds \text{s}}$$

It is useful to make three levels of forecasts: optimistic, realistic and pessimistic.

You should rank your options according to the following broad criteria:

1 The criteria of **suitability**: this is concerned with how far each option fits with the key issues identified in your situation analysis. For example, does it fully capitalize on your strengths?
2 The criteria of **feasibility**: this is concerned with whether your business has the resources and capability of carrying out the particular proposed expansion plan.
3 The criteria of **acceptability**: this is concerned with whether the option would meet your overall objectives for the business, in terms of, for example, return on capital or sales growth.

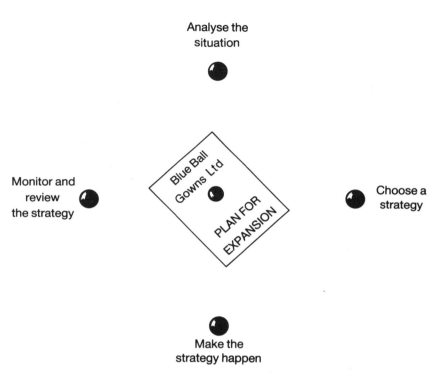

Analyse the
situation

Monitor and
review
the strategy

Blue Ball
Gowns Ltd

PLAN FOR
EXPANSION

Choose a
strategy

Make the
strategy happen

Fig. 4.2 The four stages to planning your expansion

By ranking the options in this way, you will be able to rule out any unacceptable or less attractive opportunities. For example, you may already have significant long-term loans and may be unable or unwilling to take on any significant further debt. In such cases, viable expansion opportunities would only include those which required relatively limited capital investment and/or would be likely to generate a positive cash flow in the short term. In other cases, you may have particular strengths which you want to exploit, such as an extensive distribution network or a highly skilled sales force. Clearly, in such cases, those expansion opportunities which allow you to exploit your particular strengths will be the ones you give priority to.

Making your strategy happen

The great challenge with plans is making them happen. Many businesses have business plans sitting on shelves which have been left to collect dust. Some of the reasons for non-implementation of plans include:

1 Unrealistic expectations of what can be achieved with the resources available.
2 Unrealistic time frames in which the tasks involved must be performed.
3 The lack of adequate finance to cover unforeseen contingencies.
4 The failure accurately to predict competitor responses and to plan how to cope with them.
5 The failure to communicate adequately what is required of all those involved in carrying out the plan.

You are much more likely to get your plan to happen successfully if you get: the right organization, the right people, and effective communication.

1 The right organization. You need to make sure that you are doing the right things first rather than doing things right. Once you have determined what the business should be doing in terms of tasks, then you can work out how these will be achieved most effectively. Involve your staff in developing this area. They will know better than you do how to get their tasks done effectively. However, it is your responsibility to determine what the right tasks are because of your overview and plans for the business.

2 The right people. Look at your selection processes and make sure that you haven't just always chosen staff because they are like you and who, after a few years, have left your company to set up their own small business! Make sure that your selection procedure contains a variety of factors that you will look for in potential staff. In this way you will get people who are right for their job. Check that everybody in your organization is in the right job. Take time to talk to your staff and find out their aspirations and how you can harness their motivation.

3 Effective communication. By carrying out the first two points, you will have already started this process. However, you need to make staff aware of your goals on a regular basis. One piece of research suggests that in successful companies if you ask the staff the aims of the organization they can tell you, but in unsuccessful ones they cannot.

Don't restrict your goals to long-term ones. Why not have a goal for the month or week? These can include:

a a sales target
b an improvement in production target
c a getting things up to date target
d a number of new sales calls target
e a 100 per cent return on timesheets, sales records, and so on target

Remember the success of your strategy will depend on the people working with you. Without their cooperation, nothing is possible. Spend time to inform, enthuse and motivate them. Also ensure that any fears they have are unfounded. Changes in operating policies can often lead to problems among employees who may feel their positions are threatened, and as a result may resist the changes proposed unless these are carefully explained to them.

It will help if you reduce the business plan to a series of action plans which you distribute to all involved. Make sure you talk those plans through with your staff and get their commitment to them.

Remember: if your staff are involved in developing the action plan they are more likely to be committed to it.

Monitor and review your plan

The monitoring of progress in implementing your strategy should be an ongoing process. Each stage of the strategy should be assessed as it is being implemented to ensure progress is taking place as intended. This allows any deviation from the plan to be spotted at an early stage and corrective measures taken where possible.

One aspect of control of the monitoring process is the preparation of detailed budgets for revenue and costs. A budgetary review of costs and revenues should then be carried out on a regular basis. This may involve reviews on a weekly, monthly, quarterly, half-yearly and annual basis as appropriate. Fig.4.3 overleaf suggests when some things may be reviewed.

Discrepancies between your budgeted and actual costs and revenues can then be examined to identify the causes, and where necessary corrective action taken. The monitoring process also allows you to make revisions to the plan in the light of feedback received. Almost inevitably, there will be some discrepancies between what is achieved and what was planned and these must be carefully examined to see whether the deviation is within acceptable limits.

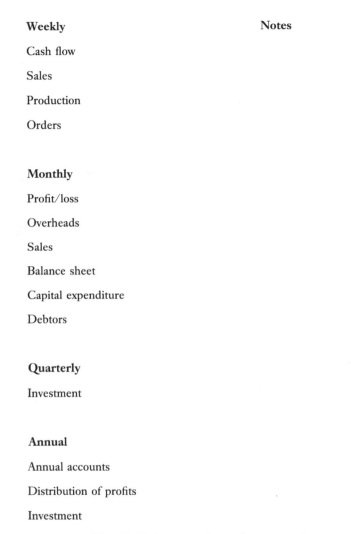

Weekly   **Notes**

Cash flow

Sales

Production

Orders

Monthly

Profit/loss

Overheads

Sales

Balance sheet

Capital expenditure

Debtors

Quarterly

Investment

Annual

Annual accounts

Distribution of profits

Investment

Fig. 4.3 Budgetary reviews of revenue and costs

An example of a business plan: Electronic Components Ltd
The following example helps to highlight the value of carefully
working through the various expansion options and, once a choice
of option has been made, of paying close attention to its
implementation.

Electronic Components Ltd, a relatively small manufacturer of electrical accessories and switches, operating predominantly in the north of England, sought to expand its business in the market for lighting accessories. The business employed some 12 people in assembling the various units, with sales made to the electrical trade through electrical wholesalers and builders merchants. The business employed two salesmen who called wholesalers and builders merchants on a regular basis. Sales to consumers were made through electrical stores and some smaller DIY stores. These stockists were contacted by both personal sales calls by the salesmen and through responses to advertising in the electrical trade press.

The business examined several expansion opportunities during the late 1980s which included:

1 Expanding sales of its existing products into the rest of the UK and particularly the south of England.

2 The introduction of a new range of 'designer' colour-coordinated lighting switches and plugs for sale to consumers and the electrical trade.

3 The purchase of the rights to distribute a range of domestic alarm systems produced by a larger French manufacturer looking for UK distributors.

The owners of the business recognized that their relatively limited resources would make it impossible to pursue all of these options simultaneously. Increasing existing sales would necessitate expanding production and would require additional sales staff, as would the development of the new product range. The chance to take on the distribution of the alarm systems was perhaps the most risky option given that they were unsure of the likely demand and degree of competition.

The first step was to carry out some basic market research into the likely demand and trade response to the launch of the new product range as well as into the market for alarm systems. This was carried out with the assistance of the local chamber of commerce and by the use of a local polytechnic business studies department, which undertook a survey of the electrical industry using students on a business studies course. This provided the basic market information that the business needed to assess the most attractive options in terms of likely demand. They were able to discount the alarm system option as it was discovered that the market was already very competitive, and the French company, being relatively unknown in the UK, would find it difficult to gain acceptance for its product. Research into the market for electrical accessories indicated that the southern market was growing steadily on the back of the building boom but that it was highly competitive and Electrical Components would find it difficult to find stockists for its standard products without offering significant discounts, that would erode its already narrow profit margins.

The reaction to the designer colour-coordinated range of accessories was very favourable. Prototypes had been shown to a number of existing stockists and potential new stockists by the salesmen and there was a strong indication that provisional orders would be forthcoming. Consumer reactions to the product had also been tested by the polytechnic study and a positive response gained.

The next stage was to estimate the likely volume of demand and hence the required production levels. Although it was impossible to make precise estimates, the owners were able to arrive at an estimate of minimum and maximum expected sales levels. This allowed them to plan the required extra production capacity that would be involved and to build this into the budget for the project.

In evaluating their sales and marketing activities it was agreed that the launch of the new range would necessitate additional salespeople, especially as it was intended to try to extend distribution to a wider range of wholesalers and retailers. It was decided that the business would recruit two new salespeople specifically to handle new accounts for the designer range and existing products. Additional promotion would be undertaken by direct mail to potential stockists and by an insert in the electrical trade press. Advertising to raise consumer awareness would be undertaken in some consumer press and a small PR company would be employed to gain editorial coverage to boost the image of the company and its new product range.

One of the partners in the business agreed to take full responsibility for the new product range to ensure the coordination of all necessary activities. A detailed plan of action was drawn up identifying:

1 All additional resources required and the funding involved.
2 A month-by-month timetable of activities to be completed, in terms of production, staff recruitment, and other activities critical to the successful launch of the product range.
3 A detailed breakdown of key retail and wholesale stockists to be contacted, broken down into sales territories for each of the salespeople.
4 A schedule of promotional activities and objectives.
5 A month-by-month budget of costs and expected revenues.

As a result of the careful planning and attention to detail, the new product development project was successfully carried through and provided the business with a significant boost to its business in both existing markets as well as gaining the business many new accounts.

Action

1 You should start off with a careful appraisal of your existing business's activity and business environment in which you operate (a SWOT analysis).
2 You should screen all potential expansion opportunities carefully against your business's strengths and weaknesses.
3 You should develop a checklist of criteria to assist you in choosing between expansion opportunities, in terms of their suitability, feasibility and acceptability.
4 The practicalities of implementation must receive particularly careful attention and contingency plans made for all possible scenarios.
5 You must keep all your staff fully informed to gain their commitment to the project. This involves taking time to talk to your staff and tell them about your goals.
6 You should draw up a detailed schedule of key activities and budgets and this should form the basis of a regular review of progress. Where necessary corrective action and revisions to the plan can then be undertaken.
7 Where unforeseen developments occur, it may be necessary to make fairly radical changes to the plan. You must always be prepared to accept this possibility, however remote, and avoid blindly following a plan that events have made obsolete.
8 When drawing up your business plan you should follow a standard outline, like that provided by 3i (Investors in Industry). Remember that the plan is not just for your potential funders but also to help you to carry out your expansion successfully.

5 Expansion of the existing business

Aims of this chapter

- To help you work out how to determine where your company's products or services stand at present in the market place
- To help you assess the potential of each of your products or services for growth
- To discuss a range of tactics that will enable you to increase the turnover of your company using your existing products or services
- To give you an insight into why profits can fall during expansion and to provide you with a number of tactics to counter this trend and increase profits

Your potential for growth

This chapter is concerned with developing your business using existing products or services and markets (sometimes known as **generic** expansion). As already shown this is usually the least risky means of expanding your business. However, for it to be a viable strategy for significant growth some conditions must be met:

1 There has to be enough sales potential in the maket to satisfy your growth objectives. For instance, the television market is not a good one for existing growth prospects as 95 per cent of households now have one.
2 Competition should not be so great that it makes any increase in sales really difficult. For instance, it is not easy to expand a General Practitioner's practice because there are so many doctors about, many of them sharing the same idea.
3 You must be able to create more capacity to meet the increased demand. Once a theatre is sold out every night, for example, further expansion is restricted by its lack of extra seats.
4 Your means of distribution must be capable of handling the extra sales or more distribution outlets must be able to be found. If your agent doesn't want to grow and has an exclusive contract for your area, then growth through existing products and markets will be virtually impossible.

5 The whole process of increasing sales must not bring the price down such that it makes the exercise unprofitable. Many construction firms win extra sales by tendering at extremely low rates only to find that they go out of business because they do not have the profit to cover the increased overheads.

From the second rule of expansion (see Chapter 3) you should have carried out a SWOT analysis of your business before choosing which method of expansion to pursue. Having chosen the existing business growth method, you will have to take a very close look at your products and markets. Let's start with the market.

Market research

In order to assess the potential for existing expansion you must find answers to the following questions:

1 What is the current size of the market: how many potential customers are there and how much will they buy?
2 What is your market share: what percentage of the total market do your present sales represent?
3 How do people buy currently, how much and how often do they buy?
4 Where, or by what means, do people buy at present?
5 How many of the recognized outlets for your product or service are you not represented in?
6 How many of your competitors' customers can you realistically expect to persuade to switch to you?

Obtaining the answers to these questions may not be easy, but here are some suggestions:

a ask your customers
b ask your sales staff
c ask anyone else who sells for your business
d look up *Yellow Pages* to see how many other firms do business in your category or similar category
e go to your local commercial library and see if there is a *Mintel* or *Keynote* report on your business sector
f look up past issues of trade journals in your industrial or commercial sector for any articles on your market
g chat to your competitors
h ask your distributors

i seek expert opinion from your local college or university

j contact *The Financial Times* to see if they have carried out a survey of your industry

k talk to your advisors: accountant, lawyer and bank manager

l contact your nearest chamber of commerce, or the economic development section of your local authority, both of which should have a great deal of information concerning the local business scene

It is best if you can carry out this research yourself, as it will give you an insight into the market in a way that no consultant's report can. However, if you simply can't find the time but you do have the money then a consultant can certainly find out information much more quickly than you are liable to. Because of their independence, they may also be able to find out information about your competitors that you may have found difficult to get. You can seek financial help through the government's Enterprise Initiative scheme – it will save you at least half the cost. Details of this and other schemes can be obtained from the DTI or your Local Enterprise Agency. Alternatively, many further education establishments such as your local technical college, polytechnic or university, are on the lookout for companies in which to place students. You can often get, for virtually nothing, a highly intelligent and marketing orientated person to help you with your research.

Hopefully your investigations will reveal lots of potential in your existing market for expansion. However, be warned, it is foolhardy to embark on a plan of attack without first carrying out your research. Too many firms have been destroyed by assuming that, for instance, they needed a bigger advertising campaign to increase sales, when market research would have shown that a simpler solution would have been to sell the product through more outlets. The result is vast expenditure with little impact on sales often leading to the company's demise. So:

 Do your research first before launching your campaign

Product analysis

There is no point in pushing a product or a service that is losing you money. Therefore, you have to examine each of your offerings to see how much you are making on them and how much potential they have for development. You need to find out the following:

1 What are the marginal costs of each product or service offering that you make, i.e. how much does it cost you to make or provide *one more* of what you sell?

This cost is called the marginal or direct cost of the product. It takes no account of overheads although it should include any costs associated with selling and distribution. The difference between this cost and your sales price is called the margin or contribution.

Let's assume that you make and sell martial arts batons. The cost of materials for each baton is £2.50. You pay your wood turner on a piece work basis: for each baton he produces you pay him £1. As you sell the batons by mail order, you have packing and postage costs associated with each sale of £1.50. Thus the total marginal cost for each baton is £5. If you sell the batons for £12.50 including postage and packing, then the margin is £7.50. Therefore, each baton you sell contributes £7.50 towards all your other costs. If all your other costs (your overheads) come to £15,000, then you will need to sell 2000 batons to break even (£15,000 ÷ £7.50). Clearly, if you manage to make the batons more cheaply, by buying from less costly suppliers or getting bulk discounts for example, you will make a larger contribution to overheads on each product. Hence you will need to sell less to break even.

Whilst marginal costing is essential for small businesses it may give rise to a false sense of security. You may feel that in order to stimulate sales you can reduce the price almost down to the marginal cost. But beware, the more you reduce the selling price the more you have to sell to break even. If you are not careful you can find yourself not covering your overheads and making substantial losses. Price cutting should be carried out with great caution and only pursued if you can still cover the overheads, either with other products or with a virtually guaranteed increase in sales that will ensure you break even. Remember, if you cut prices, others will probably respond, and you will find it increasingly difficult to sell enough products to make a profit. This lowered price soon becomes the norm and unless you have managed to see off one of your competitors and hence take most of their market share, your sales will now not be high enough to make any profits. Forcing the price up again is extremely difficult unless you now hold a substantial share of the market.

If you have two or more products or services, then by calculating the contribution for each of them, you can find out which products will give you more return for your efforts.

For example, assume that you manufacture three children's toys: a train, a doll and a jigsaw. Their selling prices and marginal costs are:

	Sales price	Marginal costs	Contribution	No. of sales	Total sales	Total contribution
Train	£13	£7.00	£6.00	1000	£13,000	£6000
Doll	£12	£7.00	£5.00	1200	£14,400	£6000
Jigsaw	£10	£3.00	£7.00	900	£9000	£6300

If you have limited resources and can only afford to promote the sales of one of the products, which should you choose? Assuming that you have no reason to believe that any one of the products will be more difficult to promote, you should choose the Jigsaw as it offers the greatest contribution per extra sale. Hence you get a greater return for your effort with this product.

If you are carrying out a service, it is often difficult to see if there are any direct costs associated with what you do. To compare how each of your service lines are doing, calculate the cost per hour or day of each of your staff who carry out the service. This is your direct cost. The difference between this cost and the income you make per hour or per day from that service line is your margin.

For example, assume you run a small marketing consultancy business with two consultants in addition to yourself. You charge £300 a day for consultancy and £250 a day for research. You calculate that the two consultants cost you £100 a day (assuming that they do 150 chargeable days a year and that they earn £15,000 per annum.) Thus the margin on either consultant is £200 on the consultancy and only £150 on the research. Clearly the consultancy is the area to try and promote. However, much of the research could be done by a less well qualified person, who could have, because they don't have to sell, more chargeable days per year. They may cost you £40 per day (£8000 per annum and 200 chargeable days.) Thus the research now has a margin of £210 and could be more lucrative to push than the consultancy, even although it brings in less money per day than the consultancy.

All this shows how important it is to calculate the margin on each product or service in order to work out which of them you should be pushing, or what you should do to make them more profitable.

2 What do your customers think of your product or service?
3 What do your competitors' customers think of your product compared to those of your competitors'?
4 What improvements could be made to your product or service?
5 What improvements and savings could be made to the way you produce your product or deliver your service?

6 What are your competitors charging for their products or services?

7 What sort of promotion are your competitors using?

8 How much of each individual product or service line are you selling at present?

9 How much is each customer or group of customers buying at present?

10 How much of your product or service range are your customers buying at present?

Obtaining answers to these questions should be reasonably straightforward:

a ask the people who sell for you

b ask your customers

c ask the people who make your product

d look at your sales records

e collect examples of your competitors' products or experience your competitors' services

f collect examples of your competitors' advertising, promotion, and sales literature

g get friends or customers to ask for quotes from your competitors or to visit them and experience how they are handled by your competitors

h ask your competitors. This is more effective if they are located in a different area and so don't feel that they are in direct competition with you

It is best if you can carry out this research yourself. However, as shown, some of the work can be done by friends or even trusted customers, and their impressions will be of great help to you. Consultants can also be used, but be careful to set out and determine exactly what you want to know and agree a set fee before they start.

One final point. You will be amazed at how much you can learn from your own workforce, particularly when it comes to improvements in procedures and methods of production. To get the best from them it is essential to involve them right from the start. Let them know where you want the company to go and your vision for the future. It is useful to ask them what they want out of work and encourage them to see how they can achieve this by helping the business get to where you want it to be.

Now that you have gathered all your information it is useful to put it into tabular form so that you can see the implications at a glance. Figs 5.1 and 5.2 suggest ways of doing this. You will, however, have to devise your own to suit your own circumstances.

Product/ service	Sales price	Margin	Average monthly sales	Average monthly no. sold	Average monthly margin	Potential for sales up	Potential cost re-duction of
1	£30	£12	£600	20	£240	High	15%
2	£45	£25	£450	10	£250	Low	2%
3	£25	£15	£1000	40	£600	None	5%
(etc)							
Totals			**£2050**	**70**	**£1090**		

Fig. 5.1 Results in tabular form: internal product analysis

Product/ service no. 1	Price	Quality	Advertising support	Market share (%)	Other comments
Our company	£30	–	£1500	5	
Competitor 1	£32	Better than us	Substantial: £2000 approx	10	Market leader: hard to shift
Competitor 2	£29	Very poor	Little: £400 approx	5	One big contract
Competitor 3	£30	Poorer than us	Substantial: £2500 approx	7	Well known in the market

Fig. 5.2 Results in tabular form: competitor analysis

Armed with all this information you should now be ready to decide what tactics you need to use in order to expand your business. There are two basic routes: building the turnover, and increasing the profit.

Building your turnover

There are several ways to build your turnover and you will probably use a combination of the following:

1 Selling efficiency and planning.
2 Advertising.
3 Public relations.
4 Sales promotion.
5 Finding new customers.
6 Distribution.
7 Product or service relaunch.
8 After sales service.
9 Customer service.
10 Direct marketing.
11 Lower prices to increase market share.

This section will examine each of these in turn.

Selling efficiency and planning

From your research you will know which customers are buying what. Your first task is to maximize the sales to this group.

1 Maximize sales to existing customers. This can be done as follows:

a Ensure that your customers are aware of your full range of products or services. For example, an advertising agency, on carrying out such an analysis of their clients, recently found that every client was unaware of some parts of their service and as a result many were placing quite considerable sums of money with other firms. Several immediately switched to the agency on finding out that they supplied a similar service.

b Try to ensure you are the sole supplier. Many organizations will happily order from several suppliers. If you find you are not the sole supplier, then offer incentives to encourage your customer to switch all their purchasing to you. Stationery firms frequently offer discount on the volume of business done with them to try to encourage companies to purchase only from them. Once you have this monopolistic position with a customer, then you can make savings on delivery and administration and eventually look to recoup your discount by slowly increasing prices.

c Maximize the use of your product or service. Your customer may simply be unaware that your offering can be used in several different ways to the one that they originally purchased it for. A leaflet containing comments from other clients who have used your product or service in different ways is often all that is needed to increase sales to that outlet.

2 Use your selling time efficiently. You must ensure that as much of your, and your salesforces' selling time is actually spent selling. Small business owners often confess to being rushed off their feet, but they can always spend an hour or two telling you about their business! Try to be conscious of the time and use it efficiently. This is best achieved by:

a Planning your sales call schedules in advance. This ensures that you minimize the distance between calls and arrive at the best time for each client. One supplier of protective clothing knew that a particular client was only ever available at 7.30 in the morning, so he started early that day and caught the customer before he disappeared for the day.

b Spending an appropriate amount of time with each customer. Make sure that more time is spent with high potential customers. One insurance broker spent huge amounts of time trying to help the small clients while virtually ignoring the big ones. When his business was eventually taken over the new owner was able to increase business by several times by spending more time on the high potential clients, whilst keeping the smaller clients happy but not spending so long with them. Many confessed to being relieved that someone new had taken over as they really couldn't afford the time that the previous owner had spent with them.

3 Set realistic goals. From the first rule of expansion you know where you want to go. You must now divide this up into manageable chunks. Work out what the turnover has to be each year to reach your goal. If it is totally unrealistic then reset your time frame or abandon the existing expansion method as a means of achieving your goal.

Approaching this from another angle, try to build up to a realistic turnover figure by:

a Setting sales targets. Agree with those that sell for you (including yourself) a sales target for the year and preferably for each month. Make sure that this is not unrealistic as there is nothing more demotivational than failing to meet your target. However, it is useful to incorporate a 'safety net' into your yearly target, perhaps by overestimating each salespersons individual yearly target by 10 per cent. This means that if one salesperson fails to make their target then the others are not put under undue strain to try to make up the shortfall in, probably by that time, the last month of the year. If you only have one salesperson, then agree the target at roughly one or two per cent more per month than you actually require, again preventing any minor slip from creating undue pressure at the end of year.

b Targeting customers. Indentify your target customers and potential customers. This will ensure you make the most efficient use of your time in relation to your goal.

c Ensuring that any company incentives will create the desired effect. For example, one small electronics firm found that their order book was increasing at a staggering rate while their production was staying almost static. On closer investigation they found that their sales people, whose bonus was being paid on order, were gaining extremely complex orders that the factory had great difficulty in producing. The sales people were saying yes to clients with complex orders because they were only interested in obtaining the order, and not in the production difficulties in realizing the order. Once the firm altered its bonus strategy (bonus to be paid when the customer paid) the problem solved itself.

Advertising

Advertising is seen by many as the be-all and end-all of increasing sales. Equally, many others see it as totally useless. The answer lies in the *appropriate* use of this promotional tool. There is no point in using advertising to boost sales if the problem is really that you don't have enough outlets. All you will be doing is making the media and, if you use one, your advertising agency richer.

Do not use advertising to boost your sales unless you know, from research, that your target market is unaware of you, or needs reminding that you are there.

You must be clear that it is a lack of awareness that is the problem before you embark on an advertising campaign. Also make sure that there is not some other, unrecognized, problem that will prevent sales from growing through your advertising.

Assuming that you have done all your checking and you are convinced that advertising is for you, the next great problem is how much to spend.

You are not alone in this. Nearly every organization, large or small, has to grapple with this question. There are a number of steps which you should follow.

Step 1: Decide a budget for advertising. This will be a combination of how much you can afford and what is realistic, in order to have an impact in the market. Past experience may have given you some idea of the effect of your advertising, but if you have previously adopted an *ad hoc* approach then it is best to start from scratch. Look at what your competitors are doing. If they continually advertise in a particular paper or magazine then the likelihood is that it is working for them. One of the most effective ways to find out how their advertising is doing is to ask them.

> A knitwear producer 'phoned up a competitor who had advertised in *Vogue* and asked how the advertisement had gone. She was amazed to find her competitor had had 2000 requests for brochures and had converted 600 of these into orders. On checking with another competitor she found slightly less spectacular but similar results. By posing as a researcher she had gained invaluable information that helped her greatly in deciding how much to spend and where to spend it.

The amount you should spend varies greatly depending on what industry you are in, but as a rough rule of thumb, 10 per cent of sales is about the average to get you started and then up to 5 per cent to keep you going. If you are in the consumer field you will probably need to spend more; if you are in a very specialist field with high costs and low margins, probably considerably less.

A word of advice. Monitor everything you do, measuring the response or reaction and learn from your mistakes and successes. Only by measuring how your advertising is doing can you hope to work out if you are spending too much or too little. Set yourself a timescale, say three months, and review how you are doing before you change anything. Small businesses have a habit of jumping from one thing to another before any have had enough time to take effect.

Step 2: Decide what the advertising has to do. Is it to create direct sales? Is it to create awareness to make it easier for your sales people? Is it to create store traffic which you then have to convert into sales? Is it to change undesirable perceptions that people may have about your product or service?

Once you have made this decision you can work out what your advertisements have to say and how they will say it. You will find that your advertising has much more impact over a longer period of time if you can keep to the same 'feel' for your advertisements. It is not just sentimentality that keeps 'Esso' using the tiger theme! Try not to imagine that you are the world's greatest copywriter. Adverts produced by the managing director almost always looks like adverts produced by the managing director: hopelessly amateur. There are plenty of designers about who can make your ad look more professional, or advertising agents who should be able to design a winning ad, provided you know exactly what you want your advertising to do and you communicate this accurately to the advertising agent (your advertising 'brief'). You may be able to get some of the costs of the design paid through the government's Better Business Scheme, details of which can be obtained from the DTI or your Local Enterprise Agency. Make sure your designer is registered with this scheme.

Step 3: Decide where you will place your advertisements. Nothing is better than experience in this area. In fact, any previous knowledge of the success of your advertising is a competitive advantage, so make sure you know what works and what doesn't. However, everyone has to start somewhere. Here are some key factors to consider:

a Coverage. This is the potential number of people who will see, hear or read your advertisement.

b Penetration. The percentage of those who see, hear or read your advertisement who are your potential customers.

c Cost-effectiveness. The relative cost of reaching each potential customer using different media. To compare different media you have to ignore the actual cost of the advertisement and look instead at the cost of reaching your potential customer. You do this by calculating the cost of reaching a thousand of them: divide the cost of the advertisement by the number of your potential customers who will see, hear, or read it. As the result usually takes the form of a fairly small number, it is customary to multiply it by a thousand, hence the term 'cost per thousand'. If it is not possible to get the figures for the number of your potential customers who will be exposed to the advertisement, then you should use the medium's readership, or audience figures instead. These are readily available from the medium's owners.

d Editorial environment. The suitability of the medium as a backdrop to your advertisement, that is, the compatibility of the content of the publication with your product or service. As a general rule, your advertising should be read, seen, or heard when the potential customer is likely to be thinking about matters associated with your product or service. For instance, you may well get to a lot of the right people by advertising your construction equipment hire service on late night television at really cheap rates, but it is unlikely that your potential customer is thinking about hiring construction equipment at that time.

Step 4: Decide what effect your advertising should have and measure it. It is a good idea to decide before your advertisements appear what response you would like. This will enable you to avoid lowering your measure of success if your campaign begins to fail to achieve what you had hoped for. If you don't reach what you set out to reach but still feel the response was worthwhile, then re-examine why and how you set your target in the first place and refine your projection techniques.

In order to decide how well your advertising has done you will have to be able to measure it. Since you have already decided what you want the campaign to do, and the level you want it to achieve, all you need to ensure is that:

a you are measuring the right thing
b you have a method for capturing the information

Simple methods for capturing information are:

1 Put a code on your reply coupon that will let you know which ad the coupon came from.

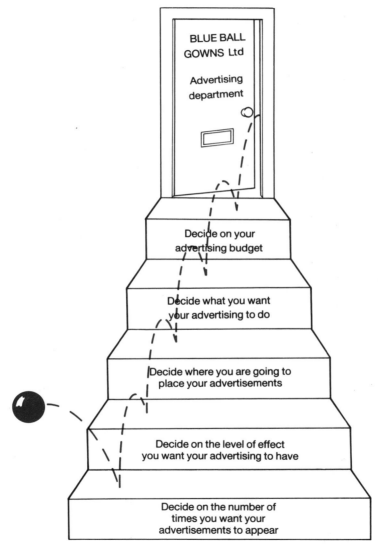

Fig. 5.3 Five steps to planning your advertising

2 Put someone in charge of collecting the information and ensuring that it is recorded.

3 Put a fictitious contact name on the advertisement and record when someone 'phones asking for that person. Everyone in your organization must be told of this and briefed as to who is to take such a call, otherwise you'll get into the awful situation of the wrong member of your staff answering the 'phone and announcing that there is no one of that name working in your company.

4 Simply ask customers how they found out about your business, and record the information.

It is important to measure not only the number of enquiries that you get from each source, but also the conversion rate of these enquiries to actual sales. The ideal small businessman could tell you the source of every enquiry to his business: whether repeat business, referral by a friend, an ad in the *Yellow Pages*, or any other part of his promotional campaign; *and* the conversion rate in terms of numbers of sales generated and the amount of money made.

Step 5: Decide the number of times you want your advertisements to appear. Again this is very much a case of trial and error, however be careful not to jump to conclusions straight after the appearance and response to your first ad. Allow two or three appearances before making a judgement. Equally, don't tie yourself to, say, six insertions of your advertisement until you are sure that it is working – no matter how great the discount.

Public relations

Public relations is often regarded as the poor man's advertising. It is certainly a much more sophisticated tool than that, however it is much cheaper than advertising if you do it yourself because you don't have to pay for the time it takes. It is also much more of a 'believable' medium than advertising.

Public relations is, however, not just about getting editorial space in the papers. It is also about trade exhibitions, special events for key buyers, sponsorship, newsletters and so on. Let's briefly look at some of these.

1 Editorial in papers and magazines. Journalists, especially those on trade journals, are desperate for information that will make their lives easier. The trick is to give them something that is newsworthy. By far the best method is to seek the help of the journalists themselves. They are much more likely to want to help someone who is struggling, than someone with a weak story but that thinks they know it all. Even if from time to time you don't succeed, keep regularly putting in the stories, and following them up with a 'phone call. You will get coverage more often than not provided you have incorporated a newsworthy item. To learn how to do this read what stories get into your target media and emulate the style and content. Remember, one good story is worth several advertisements. For example, one small gardening implements manufacturer was inundated with requests for its new hoe after a short article appeared in one of the gardening magazines. This was after a very poor response to their advertising campaign in the same magazine.

2 Trade exhibitions. For some industries, the knitwear business, for example, this is by far the best way to get new customers. However, do not go without finding out exactly who will be there, both in terms of the other exhibitors (if your competitors are going to be there then it is probably a good idea to be there as well) and who will be visiting. Ask one of the previous year's participants what it was like, as well as talking to the organizers. There are a whole host of things you need to watch about exhibitions so the best bet is to get hold of a short book on the subject and study it well before going (also see a later section of this chapter 'finding new customers').

3 Special events for key buyers. This is where you run a seminar, drinks reception or something similar, and invite key members of your target market to attend. It is important to remember it has to be something that these people want to attend. This is best checked by asking them what sort of things would interest them. General Practitioners, for example, are notoriously difficult to get to see so many companies run updating seminars on particular subjects in order to entice them along for an informal chat afterwards. Remember that these events are likely only to be attended by local people, so if your target audience ought to be head office buyers then this sort of event is a waste of time. Make sure to measure the effectiveness of these events in generating sales, although you may have to wait some time before getting any results.

4 Sponsorship. This is best avoided unless you really know what you are doing. Most small businesses make the mistake of putting all their money into sponsoring an event and then never having enough left over for effective advertising and PR back-up to have made it worth their while. As a rule of thumb you need the same amount again to get full mileage from a sponsorship event.

5 Newsletters. These are becoming increasingly popular as companies use them to spread their sales message in an editorial-type format. You don't have to have a lot of money to produce one. All you need is some useful information that your potential clients will find interesting and link this to your product or service, and you can have a one page photocopied 'briefing note' that will raise your profile with your target market.

Public relations, used properly, can be a very powerful tool for your business expansion. Get into the habit of telling the press and your potential customers of your good news when you have it.

Sales promotion

Sales promotion is basically where you attach a special offer to the product such as '10% off if you buy two', or 'a free book if you attend the seminar'. Sales promotion is used to:

1 Boost sales (and hence gain market share), for example, 'Special Summer Sale'.
2 Add value, for example, 'Free rock concert tickets with our new range of spin dryers'.
3 Encourage trial of other products in the range, for example, by attaching a sample size of a new hair conditioner to products in a beauty care range.
4 Encourage brand loyalty, for example, 'Collect ten wrappers and claim your free poster'.
5 Encourage a decision, for example, 'I can only hold this price until tomorrow'.

It is vital to cost your promotion. The following example shows the importance of this.

A small bakery wishes to encourage use of a wider range of its products, so it offers a free 'Batman' annual for every 10 wrappers from its products which must include at least three different varieties. The bakery's gross margin is 50 per cent. The annuals cost the bakery £3.00 each. The price of the products in question is 70p each. The bakery therefore makes 35p on each sale (gross margin of 50 per cent on a price of 70p.) In order to pay for each annual, the bakery must sell nearly nine extra products (£3.00 divided by the margin on one product of 35p). This suggests that the promotion must encourage a customer to buy almost nine more products than they usually do in order for the promotion to break even, let alone make money.

There are two things to note about this example:

1 The only objective this promotion would meet would be increasing market share, and this is a very expensive way to do it.

2 The number of wrappers required is too many as people don't buy bakery foods in anything like these quantities, hence it takes them a considerable time to collect the wrappers and few, if any, will stay the course.

This is a true example. The bakery in question received one request for an annual, and there was no recognizable increase in sales. Luckily they had only ordered 400 copies of the 'Batman' annual. Otherwise their loss would have been much greater. As it was they had new packaging to pay for, design and artwork costs as well as the cost of the annuals. This was an expensive mistake that could have been avoided with a little pre-planning.

An addendum to this case is that in order to increase awareness of the promotion the bakery decided to get one of its salesmen to dress up as 'Batman' and tour the stores. However, the owners of the 'Batman' copyright found out about this and informed the bakery that they were contravening copyright and that they would be sued for a considerable amount of money. Only after considerable pleadings of poverty and explanations of the highly localized nature of the promotion did the copyright holders relent. However they still insisted on the promotion being curtailed.

All this shows the importance of the golden rule of sales promotion:

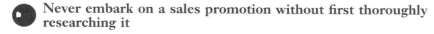

Never embark on a sales promotion without first thoroughly researching it

You need to know:
a what is your objective?
b how much will the promotion cost you?
c what increase in sales is required to break even?
d is this the most cost-effective way of achieving the objective?
e do you know how your customers will react, have you researched their reaction?
f are any hidden problems likely?

Finding new customers

Most of the techniques used for generic expansion have the objective of increasing the number of customers. It is useful to look at a few of these techniques.

1 Referrals. Every time you achieve a satisfied customer you should ask them if they know of anyone else who would be interested in your product or service. This is called the 'black spot technique'. Even if you don't succeed in finalizing a sale, you can still ask for referrals assuming that you built a relationship with the person during your efforts to sell them your product or service. In fact these are often the best referrals as the person may have a guilty conscience about not giving you an order after all your hard work. The insurance industry, for example, survives on referrals such as these.

2 Referral incentives. Some organizations offer their existing customers an incentive to suggest the names of others who might be potential customers. This is common with membership organizations, such as credit card companies. The trick is to make the customer feel that not only are they benefiting themselves but also that they are benefiting the friend or colleague. Therefore, it is important to offer an incentive to both parties; perhaps a gift for the person referring and money off for the person referred. For example, Grant card, a small local discount and credit card, offers £5 off the membership fee to the existing member and the person the member is referring.

3 Trade shows and exhibitions. For some businesses such as knitwear manufacturers and jewellery makers this is the major source of new custom. However, for all businesses there is likely to be some event at which it is worth exhibiting. These events can be a rich source of new contacts if handled correctly. You should bear in mind the following points when assessing a tradeshow or exhibition:

1 Who else is exhibiting? If similar businesses to your own then it is probable that the event is worth considering.
2 Who is likely to attend? Will there be sufficient numbers of your potential customers amongst them?
3 Talk to one of last year's exhibitors to find out what it was like and what sort of customers came round the stands.
4 Are those attending likely to be thinking about your product or service at the event? For instance, whilst there will be many people at a Highland Games meeting who will need a new washing machine, they are not likely to be thinking about that while they are at the games!
5 Is there a better event for which you should conserve your resources?

6 Let people browse round your stand. Don't stand menacingly at the front of it, daring anyone to step onto it.

7 Don't say, 'Can I help you?' Instead, engage customers in conversation about the weather, the numbers attending the event, the attractiveness of the photograph they are looking at, or anything else that will break the ice but not seem as though you are pressurizing them. This leads to the golden rule of trade fairs:

Learn from other exhibitors

Go round the other stands and act as a potential customer. Observe when you are put at your ease and when you feel pressurized. Notice what attracts you and others. Find out the best ways to display your product or service.

4 Seminars. A good way to encourage potential customers to have a look at what you can offer is to invite them to a seminar. You can either make an entrance charge or make them free, but if you have arranged for someone of note to speak then it is advisable to charge, otherwise people may feel that it is bound to be simply a sales exercise. The Dale Carnegie Foundation is an example of an organization who use this to great effect. They offer prospective clients a free seminar lasting roughly two hours during which they give a taster of what their training courses are like.

Distribution

The more widely distributed your goods or services are, the more likely you are to increase sales. For your purposes you should take distribution to cover:

a the number of outlets selling your products
b the number of agents handling your products
c the number of different ways that you get your products or services to the customer
d the range of your products or services that the outlets or agents handle

Clearly, many of the things that were discussed about increasing the number of customers and increasing the sales to each customer, apply equally well here. It is vital to realize that these outlets and agents are really your customers and you should treat them as such. You will develop your business much more quickly if you treat your distribution channels like customers, rather than suppliers. Agents, in particular, are treated in a most cavalier fashion by many firms.

One clothing firm reckoned that if the agents didn't make a near-incredible effort to get their business, then they were not worth having. This is fine if you don't want to grow, but very short-sighted if you do. So, the golden rule of distribution is:

Treat your distribution channels as customers if you want to grow

Some basic points about distribution include:

1 Do not rely on the one means of distribution. In any one area try to have at least three ways of getting to the customer. Do make sure, however, that this doesn't take business away from, say, your agent.
2 Use 'push and pull' promotional methods to get your goods or services through the distribution channel. For instance, you can 'pull' the products through by advertising and sales promotion to the end customer. But you can also 'push' them through by encouraging the agent or sales outlet, perhaps by offering incentives for increases in sales or shelf space. It is important that you find out what will motivate them. It could be the offer of bulk discounts, but it equally could be a prize of a holiday or even the chance to attend a specialist training course.

Product or service relaunch

Often sales can be increased by relaunching a particular product or service where sales have started to decline. This can be achieved through:

1 Repackaging.
2 Changing the advertising.
3 Superficially altering the product.
4 Renaming.

One other method is simply adding the word 'new'.

1 **Repackaging.** This can vary from redesigning the packaging to altering the shape of the packaging.

Hudsons International, distributers of jams and preserves, make sure that they review their packaging on a regular basis to keep their sales buoyant. They have extended their business considerably by changing the labels on their products, and renaming them, thus creating a new range of products but using the same base.

2 **Changing the advertising.** Many small businesses gain a considerable increase in sales when their advertising is taken over

by an advertising agency. The agency often brings a professionalism, or simply a change, to the existing advertising which has the effect of generating new interest in the product or service.

> The Scottish National Orchestra changed from advertising its winter series of concerts through a one colour information sheet to a multicoloured fold-out hard selling brochure. The effect was dramatic: attendances jumped from 75 per cent capacity to well over 95 per cent.

3 Superficially altering the product. This can be achieved by altering the colour or shape of the product, by increasing or decreasing the extent of the sevice, or altering the offering by any means that helps the customer perceive it in a different light. For example, by adding whisky to their marmalade, Hudsons International were able to create an apparently new product. Similarly, by changing the lecturer on a series of courses a training consultancy was able to breath new life into what had been a declining service.

4 Renaming. The simple act of calling your product or service by another name can increase sales dramatically.

> Stress Management Limited found great difficulty in selling their stress management courses until they changed their name to Leimon Taylor Consultants. Research had shown that while companies wanted Stress Management's services, they did not want to hire a company whose name clearly indicated the line of business they were in. The change of name and the use of the word 'consultants' allowed companies to hire Leimon Taylor without announcing to the world that they had a problem with stress.

After sales service

There are two aspects to after sales service, but they both revolve around the concept of keeping the customer happy after the sale. The two aspects are:

1 Maintenance of the product after sale.
2 Making sure the customer feels they have made the right choice.

Both of these lead to increased sales.

1 Maintenance of the product. As a small business owner-manager, you will probably know the phenomenon of the infamous photocopier salesman. He will be highly pressured, on commission only, male, and you might just get the odd one who makes you feel

you've got the greatest deal since sliced bread. However, although he has made the sale, it is the maintenance arrangements that determine your long-term satisfaction. It is in this area that most distributors of photocopiers fall down. Inevitably, when it comes to the intolerable stage as the machine starts to break down almost every day (or so it seems!) you look to an other firm for salvation. Poor maintenance has resulted in that particular firm losing a repeat sale.

> When John McAdams started his photocopier business, he was well aware of this phenomenon. So he decided to ensure, firstly, that he sold on quality not on price, and that he was up-front with his price, not obscuring it in copy costs or complex leasing arrangements. He gave no discounts, except if buying several photocopiers, and he always stuck to the manufacturers recommended price. His second stance was that maintenance would be second to none. He guaranteed that help calls would be answered within a specified time and trained his staff to ensure this was the case. In addition, he trained his maintenance staff to talk to the customers and keep them informed about what was happening with their machine. John's repeat business is extensive and he has grown his company on this reputation for honesty, integrity, and, above all, excellent maintenance.

John McAdams achieved success in maintenance through:

a observing what the customer wanted from maintenance, and then giving it to them
b setting standards of maintenance, in terms of responsiveness, courtesy, feedback to the client, and technical standards
c training and motivating his staff to achieve these standards

Unless you follow these points you will find your maintenance staff down-selling your organization and missing out on the opportunity of repeat sales.

The other vital aspect of maintenance is that a satisfied customer is going to sell-on your organization to others, particularly if it is a shining light in a poorly serviced sector. This word of mouth recommendation is the most potent source of increased sales for your organization. Equally, bad news travels like wildfire, and a reputation for poor maintenance is going to be a millstone around the neck of even the slickest sales operation. Do remember that a bad piece of maintenance will normally result in the dissatisfied customer telling as many as ten other people. Good maintenance, on the other hand, will result in them talking about it perhaps only to one other person. So it takes a lot of good maintenance to repair the damage of one piece of bad maintenance.

2 Making the customer feel they have made the right choice.

One of the greatest salesmen in America used to send a bunch of flowers to his customers when the new car he had sold to them was delivered. About a week later he would 'phone them to find out if they were completely satisfied with their new purchase, and then keep in touch on a regular basis each year to see if things were going well. He had learnt the secret of making the customer feel they had made the right choice.

When someone buys a product or service there is a period straight afterwards when they can doubt whether they have made the right decision. If you can give them positive reinforcement at this time then they are likely to spread the good news and hence encourage others to buy as well. This further increases their confidence that they have done the right thing since their friends and colleagues are backing up their good judgement by buying the same product or service. This reflects a basic human need to be part of the crowd. If you can help customers satisfy this need by giving them confidence that they have made the right choice, then you have a powerful technique to create positive word of mouth recommendations, as customers seek to bring more people into their crowd. You can achieve this effect by:

a Checking back. Always check back with the customer a short time after the sale to see if the product is everything that they hoped it would be. When you make a sale you often don't want to check back with the customer in case there is something wrong. However, if you do check back, and there are problems, then these can be nipped in the bud before they get out of hand and before your customer starts telling everybody what a terrible product or service you have. A useful tactic is to check back under the pretence of having another reason for calling, like delivering the maintenance record book.

> Jon Willis of Tycoon UK sells a business game similar in concept to Monopoly but with local businesses taking the spaces instead of streets. Each business gets a number of games to distribute to customers or potential customers as a promotional device. Thus every company on the game board is helping to promote every other company on the board. Jon always visits the companies a week or so after the games have been delivered to give the participating company a mounted version of the game for their wall. During this visit he is able to iron out any problems related to distributing the games and to reinforce the advantages of being involved in the project. Through this method, he has been able to ensure a happy customer base, but he has also managed to get many new referrals.

b Keeping accurate records. Always record the when, what, why and how of a customer purchase. This is the life blood of any after sales service operation. If you know when someone bought their last car, for example, then you will have a much better chance to sell them their next one if you contact them around the time when they might well be thinking of buying a new one. This also avoids the embarrassment of calling a customer when he is not in a buying frame of mind and possibly losing his favour. Remember that it is roughly thirty times easier to renew an existing customer than it is to get a new one. So it pays dividends to keep and maintain accurate records.

c Keeping in touch. Once you have accurate records you are in a position to keep in touch. This can be done in a number of ways: *Regular phone contact:* using a diary it is possible to suggest and pencil in the next call towards the end of the call you are making. *Regular invitations to events:* this keeps the company name in front of the customer but also may result in a more informal contact by 'phone or in person at the event. *Regular newsletter:* this has to be well produced and say something important. The best of these provide reviews of current thinking in areas of interest to the customer. But whatever you do, don't make it a sales document. Nothing will turn people off more quickly.

After sales service is a very important source of new and repeat business. Since it is also the seedbed for bad word of mouth, it is essential that it is given a great deal of attention.

Customer service

Customer service is something that involves everyone in your company. How often have you 'phoned a company to be appalled by the standard of telephone answering? How well do your staff answer the 'phone? This is the first impression many customers have of your business. Is it efficient yet friendly, or is it surly, uninterested, and careless? The way you and your workforce handle potential customers will determine whether they will want to do business with you and recommend you to their peers.

In the highly competitive world of today, the difference between you and your competitors may be only your standard of customer service. You can achieve higher levels of customer service by following these eight points:

1 Determine what level of customer service you want.
2 Make sure every member of staff understands this level and work with them to devise how you can achieve this standard.
3 Justify why you want this level of customer service by explaining to your staff your goals for the business and helping

them to see how they can get what they want out of work by helping the business achieve its goals.

4 Create a mission statement about customer service and keep reiterating it to the staff.

5 Constantly reward good customer service. Choose a reward and present it in a manner that will ensure that it will catch the interest and attention of the rest of staff.

6 Encourage everybody all of the time to aim for the highest level in customer service.

7 Check regularly with your customers about your customer service, and feed this back to your staff.

8 Be a shining example yourself. By treating each member of your staff like one of your customers they will be able to relate to what you are trying to get them to do.

Direct marketing

One of the most potent weapons in the small business's armoury is direct marketing. This is where you sell direct to the customer either by mail or by some form of advertising. The reason it is so potent is that it is:

1 Controllable: you can limit your sales to a manageable level.
2 Measurable: you can tell what works and what does not.
3 Targetable: so that you need only go for your particular market and not waste money trying to sell to those who definitely don't want to buy your product or service.

There are two basic ways of going about direct marketing: selling through an advertisement, and selling through the mail.

1 Selling through an advertisement. Many of the points made in the section on advertising apply equally well here. However you will need to pay particular attention to:

1 Coding your advertisements to ensure you know from which ad an enquiry comes.

2 You will usually want people to write for more details as it is often too expensive to give all the details, and put over a really good sales pitch in one advertisement. Thus it is important to code the order form that you send out with the details your customer requested, in such a way that you can tell how well each advertisement does in generating actual sales rather than just requests for brochures. For example, writing ST2 on the order form that you send out to the person who requested your brochure quoting reference ST2.

3 Ensuring you have a fool-proof system of fulfilling orders when they come in. Remember that the law requires you to deliver within 30 days or the customer is entitled to their money back.

4 Ensuring that you have a very tight administrative system to deal with the paperwork of logging the order and the money and despatching the goods. A 'daily sheet' is useful on which you can log every letter and parcel received on that day, along with details. Fig. 5.4 gives an example of how you could draw one up.

5 Selecting the media in which to place your advertisements. Do this by: finding out what their readers are like; finding where ads for similar products are placed and go for these media; finding out how the ads for similar products have gone and select the most successful media; and learning from any past experience of what media gave the best results.

6 Devising your advertisements. Again learn from your past experience as to what makes the most successful advertisements.

Date.............

From whom	Code	Cash amount	Complaint, Return, Enquiry, Order	Details	Entered on computer?	Refund, Letter, Brochure, Goods	Date

Fig. 5.4 How you could draw up your daily sheet

2 Selling through the mail. In recent years there has been an explosion in the use of direct mail, and it is often wrongly assumed that most of it ends up in the bin. Badly-targeted mailings sent out on a blanket basis are discarded, but research shows people do like to receive mailings if they are relevant to their status and needs.

Small businesses often rely on local mailings or door-to-door distribution of literature to stimulate sales both in existing markets and when trying to penetrate new markets. There are a few important rules to bear in mind:

1 Do not expect immediate results, as it is often necessary to

mail potential respondents several times before gaining a response.

2 Calculate the required number of orders you need to make the exercise cost-effective before you start – then ask yourself if this can realistically be achieved.

3 Response rates can vary on average from as low as less than 1 per cent to perhaps 10 to 12 per cent. A response rate of more than 10 per cent with a mailing to a list of people you had not tried before, would normally be exceptional. Experience is the only real guide although the people who sell lists of names and addresses may be able to advise you on possible response levels.

4 Over 70 per cent of the success of direct mail is down to the list of names used. This can be obtained by various means, for example: built up from your business's past sales records; built up from trade directories or *Yellow Pages*; using the local electoral register; or using lists from a professional list broker who will rent lists to businesses for a fee (averaging around £80 per thousand names). Names and addresses of list brokers can be obtained from:

The British Direct Marketing Association, Grosvenor Gardens House, 35 Grosvenor Gdns, London SW1W 0BS. Tel: 01 242 2254.

5 Don't get into direct mail unless you mean to do it properly. That means mailing a significant number of people or organizations with decent material. Remember the material you send to these people has to do all the selling for you, and handle all the objections. And it also means measuring all the responses and learning from experience.

6 In general, mailings to businesses have a slightly higher response rate. But the real advantage of this type of mailing is that normally there are not too many businesses to mail to. So it is possible to follow up the mailing with a 'phone call, which pushes up orders quite significantly. For example, if you 'phone a company as a follow-up to a letter you might find that the company couldn't remember what it said or might not even have read it in the first place. However, your 'phone call will jog the memory or can be used to outline the main points of the letter and create a sale where one previously didn't exist.

Lower prices to increase market share

The dangers of price cutting have already been highlighted in the section on marginal costs (see page 54). However, it is a useful strategy for building up turnover provided it is handled very carefully. The effect of a price decrease is best achieved by a 'money off' approach which allows you to resort to the original price once you have pushed up sales and your market share.

The whole point of reducing prices is twofold:

1 You hope that once competitors' customers try your product they will stick with it.
2 You hope that at least one of your competitors will withdraw from the market because of their falling sales leaving you to pick up their sales, thereby increasing your market share.

Unless you achieve either/or both of these aims, then price cutting may turn out to be throat cutting.

Monitor the effect of your price decrease closely to make sure it is having the desired effect on sales. If you intend to force a competitor out of this market then focus your efforts in their distribution strongholds. If you want customers who try your product to stay with you, then make sure the product offering is as close as possible to what they want.

Increasing your profit

The great folly of small business expansion is to become fixated with increasing the turnover.

If you are not careful this relentless pursuit will mean you will start leaving holes in other parts of your business, and you may end up with a company that is worth little or nothing. The secret is to maintain and increase your margins and to control your overheads. This can be achieved in a number of ways:

1 Production efficiency.
2 Supplier control.
3 Tight financial control.
4 Overhead control.
5 Marketing efficiency.

Production efficiency

As turnover increases many inefficiencies can creep into your production process and cause problems. This is also true if you are involved in providing a service. Basically, as pressure is put on staff to achieve higher outputs two things happen: firstly, people get into bad habits, and secondly, people don't have time to look for better ways of doing things. However, it is not just expansion that can cause production or service delivery problems. Some problems may never have been tackled since the company was formed, whilst others are a result of the idiosyncrasies of particular individuals.

The best way to tackle all of these problems is to try to get your staff to address the inefficiencies themselves. Your mission statement will have hopefully captured their imagination. If not, find out what motivates each individual and then work out with them how they can achieve that through helping the company to achieve its aims. Involve your staff in looking firstly for inefficiencies and then for solutions. This added responsibility will build morale and improve production efficiency at the same time. However, beware, you must act on suggestions or make it clear why you cannot. Otherwise you will achieve the exact opposite to your intentions. Methods to involve your staff and get the ideas flowing include:

a Suggestion schemes. These need careful planning and execution. Many firms claim that they tried this once and it did not work. The important element is to be seen to follow up every suggestion and to reward those giving them, even if it is simply a word of acknowledgement and encouragement.

b Quality circles. Essentially this involves getting groups of staff together to discuss how they can improve things and then working out a plan of action to carry out the agreed improvements. You need to take this gradually. Don't suddenly announce that every Friday you are going to have quality circles for two hours, instead let the groups form and team-build through some training. Then gradually introduce discussion on improvements, allowing the group to determine the time necessary to meet to achieve something. If you want to follow this route, it is prudent to do your research about it first or to hire an organization to help you set it up.

c Development time. Put aside some time, say an hour a week, for staff to experiment with improvements to their work. Make this time available but make the employee apply for it and explain what he or she wants to do with it. Permission to go ahead should almost always be given, since even the most crazy sounding ideas may yield something. The important point is that it motivates the person.

d Teambuilding weekends. It is possible in a small business to take everyone away for a weekend. During the weekend, a greater awareness of everybody's strengths and weaknesses can be gained. These weekends can be used to start more sharply focusing efforts by the staff to achieve the organization's goals and to devise and implement efficiency drives within particular groups.

However, the most important way of increasing efficiency is to show your staff that you care about them and to encourage them to improve, rewarding them for even the smallest move in the right direction. When asked what motivates the workers that work for them, most bosses say money and security. When the workers themselves are asked what motivates them, most say responsibility and achievement. It doesn't matter who you ask, the same sort of differing view comes across. There is a lesson here for all small businessmen.

Supplier control

Not all suppliers are the same. Some people believe you should never trust a supplier, others build strong and trusting relationships with their suppliers that last for years. However, the trusting buyer is often let down, and the uncompromising tyrant of a buyer will find he cannot get any favours when he has a problem. Not all suppliers are the same. They vary from honest to dishonest, from competent to incompetent. Each 'type' demands a different response. You need to be a different buyer to different suppliers in order to get the best from them.

	Honest	Dishonest
Competent	Demand standards but treat as equal	Must be on top of all the time
Incompetent	Coach on what you require – work with them to achieve standards	Don't deal with them

Fig.5.5 Strategies required for the different types of supplier

There is an unwritten rule that if you don't ask for something then you don't get it. In the case of suppliers this is particularly true.

The owner-manager of a small building firm was shocked when he discovered that his newly-appointed building manager was paying subcontractors the actual price they had quoted for the job. On asking him why this was the case, the building manager explained that that was the quoted amount. The owner-manager said yes, he agreed, but surely a discount had been asked for? The building manager was taken aback, he had never considered asking for a discount after the quote had been given. The owner-manager explained that if you don't ask you don't get, and that he always asked. Invariably he got 2 to 5 per cent off the quoted price just by asking and with a little haggling he often got as much as a 20 per cent discount. He concluded by stating that there was plenty of profit to be made simply by asking for it.

If you don't ask you don't get

Tight financial control

Profit can be made from getting your money in quickly and delaying your payments for as long as possible. The resultant increase in money available, or decrease in overdraft requirement, means that you can earn interest on this money, or reduce the interest you pay to your bank on your overdraft facility. For example, one small firm was able to make over £2000 in interest on money held for short periods of time before it was paid out to suppliers.

However, one word of caution. Whilst withholding payment to your suppliers can be profitable it should be tempered by the following:

1 You may build up a bad credit reference, so it is a good idea not to delay too long.
2 Don't put suppliers out of business, or put them off dealing with you. It will cost you much more than the interest made to try to build up another supplier to your ways and means of doing things.
3 Don't let your enthusiasm for getting money in ruin your relationship with your client. There are many subtle ways of speeding up payment without resorting to intimidation and unpleasantness. Many good customers are lost because of overly aggressive debt collection.

Having a tight control on spending generally is a good thing. Thus the sooner you can afford to hire a financial controller, the better. Do not forget that while you are developing your business the sheer volume of cash being generated can often obscure any lack of underlying control, and it is only when your turnover slows down that this emerges. Get your finances under control before they control you.

Some pointers towards financial control include:

1 Keep your books up to date. Daily should be the norm. In your cash book, have a bank balance column and update this with each entry so that you know at a glance exactly where you are with the bank.
2 Have monthly accounts produced, preferably by the 10th of the next month at the latest.
3 Instil a philosophy amongst your staff of questioning every expenditure as to whether: it is the most cost-effective way to achieve what they want; it is really necessary.
  Be careful though that people don't get carried away.
4 Check every invoice that comes in against a purchase order. If

you don't have a purchase order system, install one. It need only be a two part duplicate pad. Have some system that ensures that all non-overhead invoices are allocated to particular jobs or contracts and subsequently billed to clients. A simple photocopy of each invoice attached to the relevant job sheet will help.

5 Service companies should introduce some type of timesheet system to ensure that all time spent with clients is billed out, if appropriate. This will also show up inefficiencies in your working procedures.

6 Do a stock check every month at the very least, weekly if possible. Introduce some stock control system that ensures that only the most efficient amounts of stock are held in terms of production efficiency and cost.

7 Put as little money as possible through petty cash. Petty cash can become a black hole for expenditure, and can get out of control.

8 Make sure you have an annual budget that you update on a month-by-month basis.

9 Make out a cash flow, weekly for the next 8 to 12 weeks, monthly thereafter. When things get really tight, have it calculated on a daily basis for the next 6 weeks and weekly to monthly thereafter.

Remember, lack of financial control is one of the major causes of business failure.

Overhead control

It is very easy, when you are developing your business, to be caught up in the excitement of the success and not get to grips with the overheads. Remember that for every £1.00 increase in overheads you will probably need several times this increase in turnover. Equally, any saving in overheads can be added straight on to your profit figures.

The best way to handle overheads is, first and foremost, to draw up a budget for the year. You should then delegate responsibility for each budgeted overhead to a particular person. This person must keep tabs on the expenditure, planning it where appropriate, and must ensure that the business keeps to the budget, or he or she must put up a case to you or the budget group for the additional expenditure.

It is satisfying if you can keep to the budget, but if the budget was wrong in the first place then this can be a real problem. To set a realistic budget it is worth taking heed of the following points:

1 Start with past experience, not past budgets.
2 Get the person who will be responsible for the budget to set it with you. This can start with an initial budget bid and move on to a general discussion in order to arrive at a final budget amount.
3 Work out the breakeven point for this level of overheads and see if it is reasonable. Also try to compare your projected overheads with those of a similar business.
4 Now ask everyone what cost savings could be introduced to reduce the budget, and incorporate some of these but leaving a margin for error.
5 Make sure that you are seen to lead any cost-cutting exercise. For example, staff who are trying to save £10.00 on a job through obtaining numerous quotes are going to become quickly disillusioned if they see you spending £500 on a new painting for your office.
6 Show it to a friend, an advisor, and your bank manager for comments.
7 Commit the budget to paper and make sure everyone has a copy and understands its implications.

Marketing efficiency

If you want to expand successfully then you will have to carry out a lot of marketing. This will vary from looking up statistics, surveying your potential customers and revamping your brochure, to huge advertising campaigns. The only thing you can be sure of is that it is going to cost you time and money: potentially lots of money. Hence it is vital that you are as efficient as possible in this area:

1 Decide on how much you can afford to lose and work around this figure.
2 Commit yourself to a budget from the start and keep to it unless things are going so badly or so well that you are forced to change. However, do preset a trigger point for this action, for example, if sales reach 30 per cent below target for a particular month.
3 Always give consultants, designers, researchers and advertising agents a budget to work to, and draw up an agreement to say that this is all you are going to spend and that any overspending is their problem and not yours. You do not want hidden extras suddenly added on at the end.
4 Set very clear objectives as to what you want to achieve through your marketing.

5 Learn from experience and build on it. Measure everything so that you can evaluate each tactic later and learn what works best so that you can save money next time.

Action

1 Carry out a competitor analysis by finding out everything you can about your competitor, from their profitability to how they handle their staff, from what their advertisements look like to how many people they employ.
2 Carry out a market analysis by finding out what your customers think of your products/services versus your competitors' products/services. Also find out approximately how big the market is and if it is growing.
3 From the information gathered write down the areas of strength of your products/services and the areas of weakness of your competitors' products/services.
4 Bearing in mind all the points made in this chapter about building your turnover, draw up a plan of action to boost sales, including a budget, to take account of your strengths and your competitors' weaknesses.
5 Decide how you are going to maintain and increase profitability and set out a plan of action to achieve this.

6 Diversification

Aims of this chapter

- To differentiate between the three forms of diversification: pure diversification, new product development and market development.
- To help you decide if diversification is right for you and your company and examine the risks involved
- To examine and explain each of the approaches to diversification

Forms of diversification

Diversification is the process where you develop from your existing products and markets into new markets and/or new products and services. There are basically three ways of approaching diversification:

1 New products for new markets (to some people diversification refers to this area only, for our purposes it will be called pure diversification).
2 New products for existing markets (new product development).
3 New markets for existing products (market development).

The level of risk increases as you move further away from your area of knowledge and experience.

New products for new markets

Although this section is concerned with pure diversification, much of the information it contains is also relevant to the two other diversification strategies and to the whole question of whether or not diversification is the best strategy for expanding your business.

Why diversify?

There are a number of reasons why you may consider adopting a growth strategy of pure diversification. The major ones now follow.

1 Reducing risk. There is a great deal of risk associated with a restricted product or service range. The more you diversify, the more cover you have.

Liquid Levers recognized that while they had identified the garage market and produced several products that were virtually unchallenged in that market, they were still vulnerable from the fact that they only had five products. They became concerned that they were too heavily dependent on the one market with a restricted product line. Therefore, Nigel Buchanan started looking for problems that he could solve in other markets. Soon he had invented a truck tyre sensor that reduced wear and tear on truck tyres and greatly reduced the chances of a 'blowout'. Liquid Levers' diversification had reduced their reliance on a restricted product range.

2 Seasonality. If your market is heavily seasonal, diversifying into other areas will enable your company to avoid stagnant periods when machinery and staff are idle.

3 Market size. You must start thinking seriously about diversification if and when your present market becomes too small for any further growth prospects.

4 Market cycle fluctuations. Many markets experience these, for example, the building trade suffers from roughly a five year cycle.

Rectoright Preservation, a small rot and preservation firm, wanted to combat their market fluctuation and decided to also go into property development. They are now able to concentrate on this side of their business when the preservation side is in decline.

5 An aging product line. No matter how successful a product line, it will inevitably one day suffer a period of terminal decline as times change.

Robin Reid's family had been in the nuts and bolts business for years. They principally acted as middlemen between the manufacturers and the emerging African nations. However, sales had been decreasing gradually over the years as more and more of these countries started to manufacture their own. When Robin was offered the agency for some industrial strapping machines and supplies, he jumped at the chance and diversified into this product line and a home based market.

6 Faster growth. If you try expansion through your existing business operations you will discover just how slow this can be. If you require faster growth, diversification is for you.

7 Resources. If your company produces only one product or service or is particularly seasonal you can exploit your spare resources by diversifying or expanding into other areas.

The Scottish National Orchestra found that the only way they could ensure that all their players stayed with the company during the long summer gap in concerts was to pay them all year round, and so they found themselves with an orchestra with nothing to do. Their solution was to run a series of prom concerts in the summer, playing to an audience that did not normally attend their winter season, and a selection of music that they would not normally tackle.

8 Back-up. Diversification will enable you to bolster existing products or services.

By diversifying into interior landscaping (providing and looking after office plants), Findlay Clarks were able to bolster their wholesale plant business as it supplied the plants for the interior landscape division.

9 Responding to competition. It may be that you have too many competitors and the only way to grow is to move into new markets with a new line of products or services.

10 Other opportunities. You will only be able to take advantage of other opportunities if you are willing to diversify. Robin Reid (see opposite) clearly took advantage of an opportunity when it was offered to him. However the opportunity does not have to come knocking on the door, as it did in his case. If you look around closely enough you might notice a gap in the market that is too good to miss.

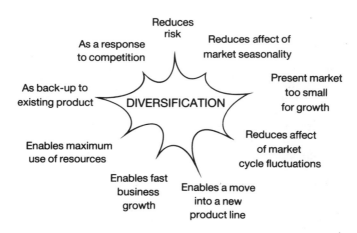

Fig. 6.1 Reasons for diversifying

The risks involved in diversification

As discussed in Chapter 3, diversification is a risky business. The main reasons for this are:

1 If it is a new market, there is a poor understanding of the customers.
2 With new products or services there has to be a lot of learning before maximum efficiency is achieved.
3 When trying an entirely new product, most organizations have to go through 200 ideas to get 20 that make it to the marketing stage, with about two succeeding. However, as a small business with a committed workforce you should be able to better that quite considerably (Liquid Levers brought all of their first five products successfully to the market) but be warned, not every good idea makes it.
4 Because there is no track record in the new market or product, financiers are much less likely to want to give help.

However, in addition to these risks there are a number of areas where the small businessman may trip up.

1 Markets. If you don't know the market you can easily overestimate its potential. On the other hand, there are many small businesses who calculate the potential correctly but never crack how to promote and sell the idea.

You can never get to know the market too well. Spend time doing *all* the research. The government's Better Business Scheme and Enterprise Initiative can help you here. You can hire a consultant under the first scheme to give you a rough overview of any marketing problems and some solutions up to a total cost of £1000 of which the government will pay half (two-thirds in some areas). Under the Enterprise Initiative, you can hire a consultant to look in much greater depth at the new market and how can you solve the marketing problems. The government will again contribute half the costs (two-thirds in some areas) of between 5 and 15 days of marketing consultancy. For details of these schemes, contact your local office of the DTI (Industry Department for Scotland in Scotland and the Welsh Industry Department in Wales), or telephone the operator and ask for *Freefone Enterprise*.

2 Suppliers. A poor knowledge of the suppliers may mean that you will buy from expensive and inexpert sources at poorly negotiated prices. Scour the country for the best suppliers and review one against another until you know everything there is to know about the supply side of the area in which you are hoping to diversify.

3 Processes. If you are not familiar with the processes of your new area production will be inefficient and beset with quality problems. Build into your budgets sufficient to get the process right before you start. The government's Enterprise Initiative can again assist here, the relevant section being the Manufacturing Initiative.

4 Commitment. If you, as the owner-manager, never really get behind the project, then it is doomed from the start. Remember, in the long run, no one gets more excited about a project than you do. You are the motivation leader. So make sure you are committed before you give the go-ahead.

5 Integration. It's an old problem that because you are too busy you don't spend the time making sure that the new team are fully integrated into the business and so petty jealousies or squabbles spring up. Do make sure that you make the time to integrate new staff and new product teams.

6 Effects on your current business. Because of mounting costs in time and money your initial business can be starved of resources and die. Alternatively, the new project overspends and eventually brings down everything. Make sure you keep to budget and be ruthless: kill it off before it kills off you.

7 Staff. By giving all your attention to the new project you might be unwillingly demotivating your staff working in your old project. Make a point of keeping the rest of your staff informed as to what is going on, and try to involve them in whatever way you can.

8 Time and money. Never underestimate this. It is often recommended to people going into this type of project: do your budgeting, double that figure and then double it again. You are probably a lot closer to the actual costs and the time spent with this figure. Quadruple your estimates of time and money.

9 Quality. Don't fall into the trap of trying to get it too right. One thing you don't want to be is a perfectionist. Too many owner-managers try to right every little imperfection in the new product, always wanting to add another improvement. By the time they get the product to the market someone else has already stolen the lion's share. As soon as you have something get out into the market place and try it. You can always improve it later. If you are test marketing properly then you should avoid any disasters.

10 Selling. Since the new product or service takes a lot of selling at the start, you must avoid diverting the selling effort from your existing lines. Make stringent and stretching targets for the existing lines and monitor performance of your new line carefully. If the new product is not going to sell then abandon it quickly.

11 'Sharks'. If your new project demands heavy expenditure beyond your means, watch that you don't become so determined to get it off the ground that you give away more than you need to. Don't sell of parts off your company to shady dealers or loan sharks in return for much needed development cash before checking that, for example, development money is available from legitimate sources merely for the price of putting together a proper business plan. You will not fall into the trap if you budget carefully at the start. Find out what the solid, dependable financial sources want in the way of figures and backed up projections and give it to them.

Help may be available towards the cost of your project from the governments's discretionary Grant Aid Scheme. Whilst you have to put up a case for the money and success is by no means automatic, companies with less than 25 employees are eligible to apply for Regional Investment Grants up to a maximum of £15,000. And you will still be eligible for other grants. For further grant opportunities see Chapter 11.

Generating ideas

Clearly you need new and different ideas in order to diversify. These don't have to be a blinding flash of inspiration, in fact for most people they won't be. You can generate new ideas in a number of ways:

1 Keeping your eyes open.
2 Getting your mind on a different track.
3 Finding problems to solve.
4 Brainstorming with other people.
5 From the workforce.

1 Keeping your eyes open. The best way to find ideas is to start looking for them. Draw a box into your diary for each day and determine to fill it every day with one idea, no matter how eccentric or unimaginative. Research proves that the greater the number of ideas you have the better the quality. You'll be amazed how quickly you start to notice things once you start this exercise. You have started to open your eyes.

Another useful technique is to make a review of all your present information sources. This must include your watching of the television and listening to the radio, as well as your reading of newspapers, journals, and so on. Once you are clear how you are spending your information gathering time at present, you can make decisions as to what to drop and what to replace it with. Try to make time to read such things as:

a broadsheet newspapers such as *The Financial Times*
b trade journals
c your local newspaper
d a business magazine
e a business book

Try also to make time to watch and listen to:

a radio and TV business programmes
b any programme that looks at different societies or looks to the future, like *Tomorrow's World*
c any programmes that deal with consumer matters, like *Watchdog*

By reviewing your sources of information and acting on the results you will be able to use your future time more efficiently by looking only at the sources of ideas that are the most valuable to you.

2 Getting your mind on a different track. People easily get locked into a particular way of thinking. They are, after all, creatures of habit. They travel the same way to work every day, hence they never see the seed of an idea that may be just a street away! But how can they get out of this mind rut? Here are some ideas to help broaden the mind:

a seek out different people at social occasions
b join a business club or your local chamber of commerce and talk to as many of the members as you can
c join professional organizations like the British Institute of Management, the Chartered Institute of Marketing, or the Institute of Export
d whenever you think of a solution to a problem, force yourself to think up two others
e if you find yourself in the habit of doing something, break it every now and again
f read a magazine that you would not normally pick up (for instance, every time you go on a plane or train journey buy a different magazine)

If you follow only some of these ideas you will find very soon that your mind will have broken free from its 'mind chains'.

3 Finding problems to solve. One of the best ways to find a winning diversification idea is to find a problem that a lot of people or organizations have and then solve it. Problems are all around us, all you have got to do is start taking note of them and you will soon have a large number to start trying to solve. It is worth asking your friends, colleagues and even people you meet in the pub what sorts of things irritate them or frustrate them about their hobby, business, home or area. You will probably be told of more problems than you thought existed!

There are lots of books on problem solving, like *Use Your Head* by Tony Buzan and *Opportunities* by Edward de Bono. However, here are a few tips:

1 Try and shift your focus of attention away from the problem. For example, the problem of people getting frustrated waiting in queues is solved by shifting your attention away from solving the waiting to the people and how to occupy them while they stand in line, thus reducing their frustration.
2 Use a random word association to help you think in different directions. For example, the problem of a lack of cash could be solved by looking up a dictionary and choosing a random word, say the third word on page seventy: 'chair'. From this you can progress through 'chairman', 'chairwoman', 'charwoman', 'cleaning' to 'washing cars in the local car park'.
3 Play off an outrageous suggestion. A crumpled shirt and no iron might prompt the outrageous suggestion of simply burning the shirt which could lead to heat – steam – boiling a kettle – putting the shirt over it to ease out the creases.

It really is true that there are no problems, merely opportunities.

4 Brainstorming with other people. Brainstorming is well known nowadays. It involves getting a group of people together to generate ideas, possibly to solve a problem or just to stimulate new strands of thought. The important aspects are:

a no one is allowed to judge ideas until the end
b no assessing the idea at this stage
c quantity rather than quality
d to select a scribe and it is often useful to have a person in the chair to keep things going and to introduce the task
e to try to have someone who is good at coming up with really eccentric ideas – they will stimulate the group to think in different directions
f do not hold back from taking a 'piggy back' on other people's ideas

Groups of six to eight are best, but you will have to try it for yourself. For some purposes you will find that having totally different and irrelevant people in the group is a good thing, while in others, especially technical areas, it is more helpful to have people that at least understand the subject.

5 From the workforce. Your workforce are often your richest source of new ideas. Again, making them feel involved is the first step. You can use such devices as:

a suggestion schemes with prizes for quality **and** quantity
b brainstorming groups
c discussion groups
d one to one interviews where you ask for ideas once you have put them at their ease
e scribble boards
f idea parties, where everyone must come with an idea and you exchange these during the evening over drinks

Remember that if you want the ideas to flow then you have to acknowledge and, at the least, reward with a word of thanks and encouragement.

Despite all this talk of generating ideas, experience suggests that most small business owners have at least one idea that they have been hatching for some time. Indeed, some have so many ideas it is as if they were going out of fashion. The problem is getting enough motivation or confidence in the idea to commit yourself to it. The next section will examine how you should do this.

How to check out your idea

Now that you have decided why you are going to diversify and you have an idea, or several ideas, how can you decide whether to spend the time and effort needed to make it happen? Basically you need to build your confidence in your idea to the level that you will make the time and find the resources. There are a number of ways of doing this, including the 'checking out' procedure (see next page): answering a series of statements which you rate how much you agree with on a scale from 0 (no confidence at all) to 5 (I totally agree with the statement: 100 per cent confidence). Try answering the statements for each of your ideas and see which comes out the highest. If you are doing this for only one idea, see how this idea scores.

Statement	Score
I think this idea is a golden opportunity	
This idea fits perfectly with my existing business	
This idea is so simple, I'm amazed no one else has thought of it	
I can fund this idea out of my existing business resources and financial contacts	
This idea will not affect my existing products and services	
I know I can get a really good margin on this idea	
The market for this idea is big enough to keep me, and any eventual competitors going for years	
I can sew up the market so that others will find it really difficult to compete	
I know exactly what channels I will use to sell the product or service	
I can think of ten people, or five businesses, I know who will definitely commit themselves to buy my new product or service even before it is ready	
I understand how to produce my idea and it presents no problem to my company	
I understand how to distribute the product and can easily set it up	
The idea satisfies a definite want in the market place	
Can I provide what the customers want at the quality they want and in the quantities they want?	
I am really committed to this idea, and am desperate to get started	
	Total score

Now that you have a total score, look at your score for each statement (if you have more than one idea, choose the idea with the highest score to look at first). How can you increase your score on that statement? By increasing your score you will give yourself more confidence in your idea and this will give you enough confidence to actually get started. You may decide that it is impossible to increase your score on particular statements. In each case you must then ask yourself if they matter that much. If you are discounting more than two or at most three statements, then you are probably going to cost yourself a lot of money and a lot of disappointment if you still decide to go ahead with your idea.

The whole point of the questions is to help you think through your idea systematically and identify those areas where you lack confidence. You will find it useful to ask yourself, 'Why did I give the score I did to that particular statement?'

How to diversify

1 Make sure you are building on rock. Unless your existing business is stable and secure, you will increase the risk of pulling the whole business down with your diversification plans. You cannot afford for your drive, enthusiasm and concentration to be diverted by troubles with the existing business. You will also need the existing business to provide stable cash flow and developmental funds for your new project. Be warned that you must sort out the problems of your existing business before embarking on your diversification plans.

2 Try to build on strengths. When selecting your idea, try to choose one that will take advantage of your existing strengths and avoid your weaknesses. If you have spare resources, try to utilize them.

It is sensible to use the expertise you already have in the business. Remember that it takes about six months for a new person to become really effective and this is one of the reasons why diversification often takes a lot longer than might be expected. If you don't have the necessary skills in-house to develop the idea then use a consultant's help. The government's Enterprise Initiative and Better Business Scheme (mentioned earlier) can assist in this area. The schemes cover half (two-thirds in some areas) the costs of a wide range of consultancy initiatives under the following headings:

The Marketing Initiative – for a marketing plan.
The Design Initiative – for expert advice on design from product concept to corporate image.
The Quality Initiative – for expert advice on how you can introduce a quality management system which meets the right standards for your kind of business.
The Manufacturing Initiative – for expert advice on manufacturing strategy and the introduction of modern methods and systems.
The Business Planning Initiative – for the development of a business plan for your business.
The Financial and Information Initiative – for budget and financial control and information systems for your business.

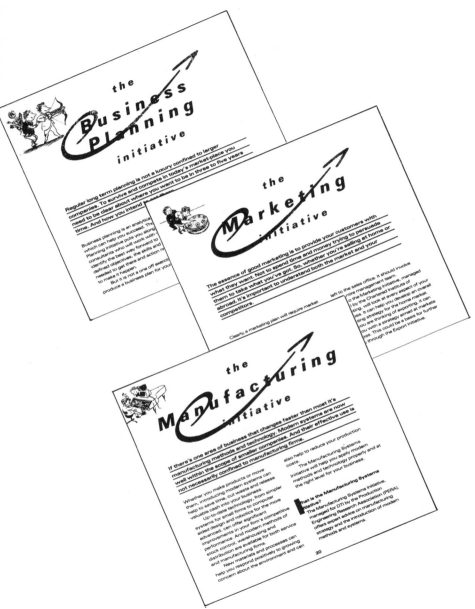

Fig. 6.2 The DTI's consultancy initiatives   Courtesy: *The DTI*

the *Quality* initiative

It doesn't matter how much time and effort you put into marketing, design and production. If the product or service doesn't live up to your customers' expectations, you're wasting your time.

If your product has to be checked constantly or sent back down the line for corrections your profits are suffering.

firm is quality minded.

And that's where the Quality Initiative comes in.

an the Quality Initiative help?

The Quality Initiative, managed for DTI he Production Engineering Research ociation (PERA) and in the North West alford University Business Services Ltd. rs expert advice on how you can oduce a quality management system ch meets the right standards – national, nmunity or international – for your kind usiness. Or how you can establish a l quality approach in all your firm's rations.

the *Financial & Information* initiative

Making the right decisions for your business means having the right information. Effective information and control systems are essential to business success.

Many businesses need independent, professional advice when it comes to systems. For smaller companies it's usually knowing where to start, while larger companies often need a strategy to bring existing systems together as the foundation for further developments.

The Financial and Information Systems Initiative offers advice on all systems which provide information on resources, production, customers and competitors. To help you control and direct

your business effectively, proven

the *Design* initiative

Look behind any successful business and you'll find that design is an integral part of its strategy. While knowing your market can help you define the product your customers want, only good design can translate it into something they will want to buy.

Design helps you meet your customers' needs for performance and reliability and meet your needs on ease of manufacture and cost.

A strategic approach to design helps position your product and your firm in the market. It doesn't matter if you're manufacturing luxury goods or serving the mass market. The story is the same.

Even if your product is up to scratch now, you will have to ensure it evolves to meet new demands, such as increasing concern about environmental issues, and opportunities such as the Single Market.

If the market doesn't recognise what

you're offering, you're not fulfilling your potential.

ow can the Design Initiative help?

The Design Initiative, managed for the DTI by the Design Council, offers expert advice on design from product concept to point of sale. It can also help you improve your firm's overall approach to design management.

Amongst other things, you can get help with:
- product innovation and feasibility studies
- design for efficient production
- design for performance and reliability

18

For all of these initiatives, you should contact your local DTI office or Enterprise Agency. The Department of Trade and Industry (ring them on *Freefone Enterprise*) will give you a local contact if you cannot find one. The DTI also offers grants to help you with developing innovations. The Regional Innovation Grant will cover half of the cost of the development of your innovation up to a ceiling of £25,000, provided your business is in a Development Area, is independent, and employs less than 25 people. Make sure you investigate all the possibilities. Your accountant should be able to help, but don't rely on him or her knowing about all the schemes that are on offer.

3 Get motivated. Use the checking out procedure described on page 94 to help you get motivated. The more positively you can respond to each of the statements the more motivated you will become. If you come across a setback don't stop, solve it! Remember, 80 per cent of new sales are made after the fifth sales call. This statistic applies equally well to finding ways round problems. If at first you find yourself facing a discouraging problem try at least five ways to get round it before you call it a day. For example, Colonel Saunders of Kentucky Fried Chicken fame tried over a thousand outlets before he got one to try his new recipe for cooking chicken. When would you have stopped?

Surround yourself with positive people. If someone you normally discuss things with is negative about your idea, find someone who sees the good points about it to chat to. It is hard enough keeping your own spirits up without someone trying to dampen what little flame you have. Walt Disney always maintained that if all his advisors thought one of his ideas was no good, then it must be a winner and he would ignore all of them and do it anyway. Having said this, you have to be sensible and the checking out procedure will help keep your feet on the ground without demotivating you.

4 Make sure the market is right. If you want to succeed then you must find out:

    a who will be your customers?
    b what are they like?
    c what changes to the product or service would make them even more enthusiastic?
    d how best can you sell to them?
    e how many will they buy and for how much?

You will find lots of books on do-it-yourself market research, or buy *Successful Marketing for Small Businesses*, a companion volume in this series. However, the most important point to remember is that there is nothing to beat speaking to your potential customers in person about your product or service. You will learn more about the weaknesses and strengths of your idea from five chats to potential customers than a whole lot of formal market research. One way of doing this is to set up your own MI5 (Market Intelligence Five) Group. The MI5 Group is a method of getting to know a new market intimately. Identify five individuals who are in the target market or who buy for companies in the target market and get to know them so well that you can call them close friends. By understanding how they think and react, you will understand your new market. By keeping in touch with your MI5 Group, you will become aware of any changes in the market swiftly and without expensive market research techniques.

The more you can pre-sell your idea the better. Not only does it bolster your confidence that it will actually work, but it also provides you with a spur to get on with it. For instance, working in conjunction with a major customer from the start in order to tailor the product to suit them is very useful. They become committed to take it when it is produced, and worries about the sales success of the project are solved even before you begin.

5 Budget generously. Diversification projects invariably cost more than you expect. It is therefore vital to work out what you can afford to lose, and budget from there. The budget must be as generous as possible: when you are developing a new product or service you are bound to hit snags. Chapter 11 covers this subject in more detail.

6 Have a plan of action. The big companies work out a critical path analysis for their diversification projects, where they calculate which operations have to happen first so that other operations can lead on from them. In other words they plan ahead. Without a plan of action and timescales that everybody knows and agrees with, you can find yourself beaten to the market by a competitor. You should follow a standard plan as shown in fig. 6.3 overleaf. Some of the main features of the plan are:

a Idea screening. Where you have a number of ideas and you choose between them, eliminating at this stage the ones that you don't feel will work after you have completed the checking out procedure.

b Initial checking out. The examination of each individual checking out statement to help refine your idea.

c The one page feasibility study. Where you make guestimates as to how many you might sell at what price and what it would cost you

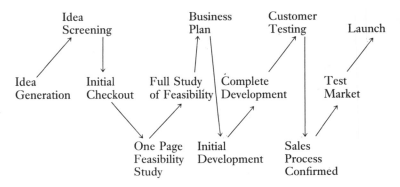

Fig. 6.3 A plan of action

to produce and sell them. This is like a rough profit/loss calculation. It gives you a figure which will show you whether it is worth proceeding or not.

d Customer testing. When you have a prototype and you get potential customers to try it out and talk about it. Their comments will help you produce an end product that sells.

e Test marketing. Where you actually market the product in a restricted area to see how it will go. This reduces your financial exposure if it turns out to be a flop.

At each stage of fig. 6.3 you should set criteria beforehand to determine whether you should continue with the project at that stage. If the project fails the criteria (for example, a production cost of 30 per cent of the recognized selling price) at any stage, this does not necessarily mean that it should be killed off. You will however need to take a very careful look at the project. You may have to spend some time attempting to get the idea to pass the criteria.

7 Encourage positive thinking. If you are going to get your idea to the market at a fraction of the cost of what it would cost a large business, then you have to have everybody that is working on the project at a fever pitch of commitment. Encourage everyone to think positively. Prevent people from pulling holes in the project without also putting forward positive solutions to fill the gaps. Let people make mistakes. They will learn far more by trying things out than by being restricted by your supposed superior knowledge. Even so, you can still gently guide them down your solution route.

If you want people to be creative you have got to give them room.

New product development

You may feel that all the risks and pitfalls of pure diversification are too great and you want to restrict yourself to developing new products for your existing markets. You can pursue new product development as follows:

1 Improving existing products.
2 Replacing existing products with new ones.
3 New products that extend the range but utilizing the existing sales channels. For instance, a bakery developing a new line in shortbread, which it sells through the small retail outlets that sell its existing products.
4 New range of products but utilizing the same sales channels. For instance, a bakery might produce ready to bake, just add water, cake mixes which could be sold through the retail outlets that it already supplies with bakery goods.
5 New products through new sales channels but to the existing market. For instance, supplying the ready-mix cake product to supermarkets.

The advantages and disadvantages of new product development

The main advantage with this form of diversification is that by keeping to the same market, you reduce the risk of failure, since you already know your customer intimately. Intuitively you will move in the right direction because, if you are working on a stable base, this only derives from really knowing your customer well.

Another advantage is that new product development is easier to finance than pure diversification since you have a track record to play on and you can demonstrate a thorough knowledge of the market. Also, there may well be some synergy between the existing product line and the new product since as you are aiming at the same market the new product may help sales of the existing product line. One final advantage is that because of your knowledge of the customer this leads to better designed products and more informed and realistic pricing.

The disadvantages are the same as for pure diversification but the risk is less because you already know the customer and the basic selling processes.

The key is to try to keep as close as you can to your existing production skills and resources.

Some key points on how to go about it

As one of the methods of diversification, this chapter has already broadly covered how to go about new product development. Fig. 6.3 provides the basic plan of action. However, there are a few key points that you should consider about new product development.

1 Customers. Use your customers to help you generate new ideas. This may take the form of creating focus groups to chat about the existing products, how they are used and what would be useful to have in addition. Or you may want to form regular brainstorming groups for product discussion sessions. In addition, salespeople should be encouraged to talk to customers to find out what products they feel they would find useful but aren't available in the market place.

2 Research and development. Cut your research and development time to a minimum by keeping as close as you can to your existing strengths. Make sure however, that the projects your staff are working on are market led and not just a technically brilliant, but unsaleable product.

3 Resources. Use your existing production resources if at all possible so that your staff do not have to learn the vagaries of many new machines.

4 Reaching the market. Sell through your existing sales channels if at all possible. This way you can pre-sell your first production run. This has obvious advantages for your cash flow, but it also gives your bank tremendous confidence in your new product ideas.

5 Promotion. Use an existing line to promote the sales of the new product and vice versa. So, try to build in some sort of relationship between them.

> When TMS Advertising, a small advertising agency, wanted to diversify into a new area, they had to decide between public relations or marketing as the area to put their resources behind. In the end they opted for marketing because there was a direct link between this and their existing line of advertising. Any marketing client would have need of the advertising side once the marketing plan was devised, and each advertising client was encouraged to look at marketing in order to get their advertising more clearly focused. Public relations, on the other hand, was seen as an alternative to advertising in most of the small firms in which TMS were operating, thus there would have been little or no link. This meant TMS would have made precious little in the way of extra business with existing clients. Equally new public relations clients would have generated little in the way of advertising.

6 Sales. The more new products that will make a profit based on conservative sales to existing customers, the better. If you can start from this base then you will have a much greater chance of success. For example, Liquid Levers were able to move confidently into their second product (see previous case studies), because they knew that only a modest percentage of those who had bought their brake bleeder would also need to buy the hydrolastic suspension machine for it to break even.

7 Competition. Try to avoid going into products that have direct competitors, unless you have significantly improved the product or the production method and hence the price.

8 Product perspective. Even if it is a pet project, put your new product into the proper perspective. If it looks like it is going to fail, kill the project off rather than have it gradually drag down the company in terms of cash and morale.

Market development

You may feel that the failure rate of developing new products is too high for you and you wish simply to find new markets for your existing products. While this is an appealing strategy as it sticks to the processes you know and understand, do not underestimate that there are risks involved.

One of the main risks is that since there are little capital or development costs involved in this strategy, new market development can quickly use up your finances in a most unsuspecting way.

In their search for new people to train as weight control instructors, Weight Management advertised in many different places. Because they had not researched the market fully before starting on their promotion, much of the advertising was wasted. More and more money was lost as the company tried to find a new market. By the end of the year a huge sum had been spent, not just in advertising, but in staff time, new literature and so on.

So, without a clear plan of action, new market development can be as risky as new product development.

Most of the tactics required for market development have already been covered in the discussions on generic growth (Chapter 5) and in earlier sections of this chapter. However, it is useful to look in detail at some specific challenges associated with this type of diversification strategy.

Different types of market development

There are several different ways of achieving market development. These are geographic, by use, and by user.

1 Geographic. The further away from your own area the more difficult it is to succeed. Expanding in your own country must be your first aim. This is handled by:

1 Appointing agents to cover new areas.
2 Setting up satellite operations in new areas. This is not highly recommended as there are a lot of control problems involved. However, it is an option.
3 Expanding your distribution system and increasing your promotion accordingly. This may involve new staff and it can be useful to consider local people in the new area to help you with local knowledge and contacts.
4 Devolving the selling to a distributor in the area. This may be someone who is already selling to your type of customer in that area.

Any further expansion involves exporting and this is a whole new area in itself. This area has been well covered in a companion book in this series, *Successful Exporting for Small Businesses,* so it will not be covered in depth. However, a few important points are worth mentioning.

Do not consider exporting seriously until you are established in the UK. Although there are some products that are particularly suited, for instance, to the American market while there may be little demand in the UK, you should not in general get diverted from your primary task of establishing yourself in the UK.

If you are ready to export then make sure that you assess each potential foreign market before moving into it. It is much better to concentrate on one country at a time and gradually build out from that established base. If you are serious about making a success of exporting then you will need to develop an export marketing strategy which should include the following:

a what is the market size in your target countries?
b who are your main competitors?
c what shares of the market do they have and how do they market themselves as far as price, product quality, promotion and distribution are concerned?
d how will you have to alter your product offering to suit the market?
e are there any government regulations that will have an influence on your product?

f how will you cope with the extra administration?
g how will you sell in your target markets?
h what will be your method of distribution?
i how will you monitor any agent or distributor you are using?
j how will you cope with breakdowns and faulty goods?
k how well do you understand the culture and language?
l by what means will you expect payment?

From this analysis you will be able to choose the best country to start off with and what your strategy to extend to other countries will be. This will prevent you from falling into the trap of simply going for the country that has shown the most interest rather than the one that is identified through careful research and analysis.

If you want to read further on this subject, your first call should be to refer to the books mentioned in the further reading list on page 171.

2 By use. It is quite possible to extend the sales of your product if you can find new uses for it.

A hand cream company, when it surveyed its customers about their use of the product, found that only 30 per cent were using it as a hand cream. 30 per cent were using it as a sun barrier cream and 40 per cent were using it as a facial cleanser. The company had no idea that there were these other uses for their product.

New uses can be found by:

1 Asking customers what they use the product for.
2 'Brainstorming' sessions to gain ideas. This can either be with a group of your staff or a group of users. The techniques are the same as those used for trying to gain new product ideas but in this case you have a particular issue that will require more relevant and constrained thoughts and ideas. Cue statements like 'see it from another person's point of view', and 'try looking at the negative of what you are discussing', can be devised to help the group get out of particular ruts of thought.
3 Running a competition, amongst users, of their ideas for new uses for the product.

The great advantage of this form of market development is that it often retains the existing users as the target market. This means that your already established sales channels can be used. Since you know the customers it is easy to promote and sell to them.

3 By user. Finding new users is difficult. A few techniques include:

1 Analyse your customers to see if any new user groups are emerging. If it is an industrial product this can be done by

asking on your product or service order form what the company (customer) does. For other products some form of research will be required. Take a random sample of your customers on a regular basis and contact them to discover what groups they come from. If it is possible to quiz the customer at point of purchase then this should be formalized and results produced each week.

2 Brainstorm, once again with members of staff, or a group of creative thinkers, or just different thinkers, assembled for your purpose.

3 Keep asking your contacts if they can think of any new markets you could tackle with this product.

Given that you are dealing with a completely new set of customers with this form of expansion, it is necessary to put together an MI5 Group (see page 99) to help you to get to know how to tackle them. You may find you have to use a new sales channel such as direct mail or telesales.

This form of market development demands changes to your method of promotion so that it appeals to the new target market. Since this market is totally new to you, this strategy is bound to be a riskier proposition than, say, the geographic expansion in the UK strategy. However, the drawbacks and pitfalls are similar to those faced when considering the exporting strategy.

Two final points

Consider structure

You want to get clear in your own mind fairly early on how you are going to structure your type of diversification. For example, if your diversification strategy involves a new product is the new product area going to be:

a made into a subsidiary company?
b a total subcontract operation?
c housed in a different unit?
d produced and sold by existing staff?
e licensed out to someone else to produce and sell?
f financed as part of the existing business or as a separate project?

Integrate fast

As soon as your new project is up and running it is essential to integrate it into your existing business as fast as possible. Otherwise petty jealousies start appearing and this can be very damaging to the business as a whole. The only alternative, of course, is to separate it off completely.

Diversification, despite all its drawbacks, is a tremendously exciting area to work in, especially if you are investigating new ideas. But do be careful that your excitement is tempered by a plan of action and some realism.

Action

1 Draw an ideas box into every date in your diary. Jot down an idea into the box each day.
2 Assessing the risk and growth implications, decide which form of diversification you which to pursue:
   a pure diversification
   b new product development
   c market development
3 Build your MI5 Group for each new market you intend to enter.
4 Write down any ideas you have at the moment and test them against the checking out procedure.
5 Draw up a plan of action and budget for your diversification, in rough form initially (one page A4) and then develop it.
6 Decide what your cut-off points are going to be, at which you will abandon the project if it fails to meet your criteria.

7 Acquisition

Aims of this chapter

- To introduce you to the concept of acquisition
- To help you choose the right type of company to acquire
- To give you a system to choose between possible candidate companies
- To help you build up a plan of action for acquisition

An introduction to acquisition

Acquisition, the acquiring of one business by another, can be seen as a speeded up version of all the forms of growth that we have looked at so far. It can remove all the research and development that the other routes demand. This is achieved through taking over another business that already has:

a market share in your market (generic growth)
b the same products but is operating in a different market (market development)
c other products that would sell in your market (product development)
d other products that sell in different markets to yours (pure diversification)

So why doesn't everybody go down this route as it seems so much simpler? It is because there are a number of major problems associated with acquisition, and they will be covered later. However, some of the more important considerations are:

1 It is not simple. Typically, negotiations can take up to a year or more to complete.
2 The failure rate is high. Recent research in this area suggests that up to around 70 per cent of acquisitions fail to live up to the expectations of the buyer, although many accountancy firms claim that the actual failure rate is lower than that of new businesses.
3 Supply and demand. There simply may not be any suitable businesses around.
4 It can be more difficult to finance. Although there are ways round this, your exposure tends to be higher and without the

psychological comfort of knowing that you started from scratch and know exactly what you are doing.

Despite these reservations, it is possible to succeed. This chapter examines how you can grow through acquisition without losing everything along the way.

Choosing the right company

Acquisition is an accelerated route to growth. A look at fig. 7.1 will help you decide what type of business would be the most suitable for you to acquire.

Your company's problem	The company you should acquire
No more capacity	Competitor, or company with similar production process, with plenty of spare capacity
Spare management time	Poorly managed business
No obvious successor to owner-manager	Company in your field with dynamic and talented young owner
Market is saturated and growing slowly or declining	Business in younger growing market
Growing too slowly through generic expansion	Competitor
Good sales channels with underused potential	Business supplying complementary products or services that can be sold using your sales channels
Concern over continuity of supplies	Key suppliers
Concern over retaining customer who may fail, be acquired, or be looking for another supplier	The customer in question
Spare capacity	Business with good customer base whose production can be transferred to your premises
Bored with present business	Any business that will rekindle your enthusiasm for it and your existing business
Lack of new technology	Business that has it (probably failing because of the cost of development)

Fig. 7.1 The relationship between the needs of your company and how acquisition of the right company can be of benefit

By matching the attributes of the target company closely to your needs, you increase the benefit of buying the business whilst decreasing the chances of failure.

A plan of action for acquisition

As with all the other methods of expansion, a plan of action helps organize your thinking and the order of your tasks. There are ten steps to successful acquisition:

1 Decide what type of company you want.
2 Select at least three target companies.
3 Get to know as much about them that you can.
4 Select the best and make an informal approach about combining operations.
5 Find out what they want and help them achieve it through the acquisition.
6 Organize finance.
7 Start negotiations.
8 Agree sale.
9 Immediately reassure staff of both companies.
10 Be seen in the new operation and the existing one.

1 **Decide what type of company you want.** Using fig. 7.1 you can get a rough idea of the type and nature of your target company. This is probably sufficient to start your search, but it is useful to set out at the start what criteria you would regard as the **perfect** match. You can then compile a grid and rate each of the target companies against these criteria to see where they are deficient. Your grid might look something like the one shown in fig. 7.2.

Criteria	Your preference	Rating (out of 10)		
		Company 1	Company 2	Company 3
Size	15 staff	7	6	9
Industry	Wholefood baking	8	9	9
Market share	5 per cent	4	9	7
Location	Within 5 miles	9	3	7
Management	Poor	5	5	2
Turnover	£450,000	7	4	9
Premises	Modern	1	4	8
Customers	Different to ours	9	5	2
Products	High quality	2	5	9
Totals		52	50	62

Fig. 7.2 Calculating the perfect match

From fig. 7.2 you can see that company number three comes out the best. However, that may still not make that company your automatic choice. You may particularly want as different a customer base as possible, and company three has a very similar customer base to yourself. So you may decide that, initially anyway, it is better to pursue company one because they have this different customer base you so particularly want.

Fig. 7.2 is very useful for helping you think through your reasons for acquiring a particular company. You will choose criteria to fit your situation, effectively creating a 'specification sheet' for the ideal target company.

2 Select at least three target companies. The reason for three or more companies is because this way you will have some means of comparison, which will illuminate your views on your preferred option. If you only have one company in your sights, you may well compromise on your criteria, which could lead to disaster later on. Your targets need not be limited companies, although this is the most likely option. They can be sole tradeships or partnerships, but are unlikely to be quoted companies with their shares on the Stock Exchange (although anything is possible).

Finding potential candidates for purchase can be tricky. There are 'Businesses for Sale' columns in regional and some national papers, notably *The Financial Times*. Be careful though, they are selling for a reason, and you must make sure you are aware of this reason. Keeping your ear to the ground locally will help, but a quiet word in a supplier's ear will often throw up some interesting information. However, don't assume that you can only acquire a company that is on sale. Some of the best buys are from people who had not considered selling until someone else had put the proposal to them. If you are that keen to take over a particular company, put in an offer and make sure that the owner knows you might be willing to negotiate. The chances are that you will get the company you particularly want.

3 Get to know as much about them that you can. You need information to fill in your version of fig. 7.2. This can come from a number of sources, although you will need to be a bit of a detective. It can be great fun playing the amateur private eye, but make sure your analysis is professional. Sources of information include:

a customers
b suppliers
c credit reference organizations
d your bank

e your professional advisors
f Companies House for their accounts and shareholdings
g neighbouring businesses
h their trade organization
i local newspaper people
j the editor of their trade magazine
k business clubs
l mutual contacts

Remember you also want to find out how they tick: where does the power lie? Who are the shareholders that you have to win over? Who influences their thinking? What are their staff like? And so on.

4 Make informal approaches about combining operations. Nobody likes to be 'taken over', so it is useful to start off with the more sensitive approach of 'combining operations'. This is, of course, irrelevant if the business is already up for sale. How you approach this is very much a question of your own personality. Approaches can vary from simply walking into the premises, speaking to the owner and asking how much he wants for his business, to writing a letter enquiring about the possibilities of arranging a meeting in order to chat about something that might be mutually advantageous.

5 Find out what they want and help them to achieve it through the acquisition. You ought to treat a potential acquisition as making a very complex sale. So, just like the good salesperson, you should listen as much as possible. Find out what interests them and motivates them. Maybe it is something outside work that your purchase of their shares will help them to achieve. Maybe they don't like the financial responsibility of total ownership and would respond to a small share of a bigger operation. Maybe they never realized how much their company was worth and what they could do with the money. By finding either the, or a, reason for selling could give you the leverage to consummate the deal quickly and to everyone's advantage.

6 Organize finance. You will probably have had informal talks with various sources of finance before you get to this stage, and although the negotiating of finance goes on throughout the acquisition process, the main thrust probably comes here.

Your first port of call must be your own bank. They know you and your track record. This may or may not be a good point. If the latter is the case, try another bank. You quite often find that some banks are much more keen to lend on certain propositions than others, because of their experience in the area or a desire to become involved in that industry. The next in line are the merchant banks. Your bank will have a merchant bank arm so why not try them first, if only to get your pitch sorted out. If you have a pension fund, it may be possible to borrow against it. Personal insurance and pension plans may help if this is to be a personal rather than company acquisition. Be wary in this area however, as interest rates tend to be high.

It may be necessary to turn to the venture capitalists for help. Investors in Industry (3i) are probably the best known in this field. Contact them at:

3i, 91 Waterloo Rd, London SE1 8XP. Tel: 01 928 7822.

Further details about other venture capital organizations can be obtained from:

The British Venture Capital Association, 1 Surrey St, London WC2R 2PS. Tel: 01 836 5702.

Your accountant or solicitor can also put you in touch with these organizations. They make most of their profit from an increase in value of their money (mostly invested in some form of shares). However, this can only happen if there is a buyer for their shares in the future. So you may have to convince them that the acquisition is going to lead to a large and rapid increase in the value of their shares and that you intend to go public in the not too distant future, or will have the wherewithal to buy back the shares at their increased value. Venture capitalists tend to look for something in the region of 25 per cent return on their investment initially, with a ten times return in five years. But remember, everything is negotiable and they are the suppliers, so get the best deal possible and on as near your terms as you can. Don't forget, if you don't ask you won't get.

You will probably want to fund some, if not all, of the investment from your existing business's resources. Some sources of financing from your own business are:

a stretching suppliers
b very tight credit control
c factoring your debts
d refinance equipment or premises
e sell and lease back premises
f sell off non-essential equipment
g reduce stocks
h sell shares to your staff

It is possible to get the business you are acquiring to fund a proportion of the cost. The principals can be paid over a number of years with amounts tied to profitability. The principals may be

Fig. 7.3 Organizing finance: the first place to turn for help is your bank

encouraged to treat the purchase price as a loan to you at fairly attractive rates, that are still below the rate you would be charged for a commercial loan.

The assets of the target company can be used as collateral for a loan or simply sold to pay the sellers. This is known as a leveraged buyout. For example, a small firm could be purchased with cash raised on the strength of its stocks, and delayed payments made to the sellers from the proceeds of selling that stock. However, leveraged buyouts are tricky and you'll need good legal advice, especially to avoid any likelihood of personal liability should things go wrong. Many larger lawyers now have partners who specialize in this type of company buyout.

7 Start negotiations. If the company you hope to acquire accepts your first offer then your offer is probably too high. There may be problems with the company you don't know about, or your price may simply be higher than they expected. Remember, the best negotiations are the ones where both parties win. You never know when you have to seek the seller's help in the future. Equally, he or she may be working for you after the sale so it is worth keeping on their side. Try always to put yourself in the other person's shoes. It is worth reading *Getting to Yes* by Roger Fisher and William Ury, or *Everything is Negotiable* by Gavin Kennedy, to give you an insight into the art of negotiation before you start your own.

8 Agree sale. While this may seem straightforward enough, you must ensure that there are no holes in the agreement, so this is where your professional advisors come into their own. Your solicitors should draw up the agreement. Make sure they are experienced in that sort of thing – the family lawyer will not do. Get a specialist, if you are at all in doubt, it will save you in the end.

Your accountant needs to make sure of the tax implications. It is too easy to make a mistake that could have quite radical implications in the future. You don't want to get into the situation experienced by one company, which took over another, ailing one and found to its horror that a year later only 50 per cent of the ailing company's losses could be claimed against tax, because of the way the purchase was structured.

9 Immediately reassure staff of both companies. As soon as the sale is agreed, you must reassure the staff of your target firm. There is nothing more invidious than rumours of sale and confirmation without further information. The good staff are the first to leave as they can find jobs quickly and if you are not careful you may lose that which you bought the company for. As soon as you take over arrange to have individual chats with each member of staff. This allows you to assess them and to reassure the ones you want to keep of their importance and central role to your plans. You may have to negotiate new terms with them, so make sure you are properly prepared.

While all this is going on, your existing staff will start to worry if you don't act to maintain confidence by keeping them informed. Key members of staff who could possibly be affected by the purchase should be met individually and drawn into your plans. It is also best to check on any other key individuals who won't be affected by the acquisition, as rumours spread like wildfire and you will want to reassure them.

10 Be seen in the new operation and the existing one. The fact that the boss is about helps to calm fears. It also ensures that things are going according to plan. This is not the time for a Caribbean cruise! People need to be able to talk to you and to feel that you care about what they are doing. More so than at any other time, people will want to impress you. If they don't get that chance, then they may feel that they are not valued and leave. You also need to be seen to let everyone know who is in charge. You need to encourage and communicate your vision of the future. At a time of flux, such as this, people need very strong direction. Many of the real benefits of acquisition have been lost at this stage through entrepreneurs spending their time crowing over their buying-out success, and failing to realize that their real chances of long-term success are beginning to drift away from them.

How much to offer

There is no correct answer to this question. The seller will probably value the business on the future profits that it is likely to make. A rough rule of thumb is to offer ten times the last three years' average profit. However, you may decide that you want to value the business on its present asset value. Whatever the formula, the only real answer is what the seller is willing to accept. Remember, you can alter the terms of payment in ways that will not affect the seller but will make a big difference to you. For instance, in order to minimize their capital gains tax payment you may ask the seller to consider part sales over a period of time, which would benefit your ability to finance the deal. When calculating your return on investment you will want to calculate the likely future profits of the combined operation over your existing business's plans. To get a true view of this you will have to take account of interest rates and inflation in your calculations. Details of the financial implications of expansion will be found in a later chapter of the book (Chapter 11).

Problems associated with acquisition

As already stated a high proportion of acquisitions do not live up to expectations. There now follow a few of these problems, which, if solved, may help to reduce the chances of dissatisfaction:

1 Overvalued assets.
2 Sales bolstered by unprofitable prices.
3 Sales bolstered by operation owned but not sold by the seller.
4 Major customers about to go elsewhere.

> A small advertising agency thought they had a good deal when they bought over a local public relations firm, only to find once the deal was completed that the major customer was going to take its public relations in-house. The sellers had been well aware of this and was one of the reasons they were keen to sell.

5 Reduced motivation of the principals of the company being sold after acquisition. Make sure you keep the principals of the selling company motivated, if they are vital to the operation, and that means finding out what motivates them.

> An estate agency was taken over by a large financial institution. The deal involved the principals of the agency receiving several million pounds each over five years, depending on profitability. After the first year, the principals had so much money that they lost interest in maximizing profits and were off indulging in new projects.

6 Falling market.

> Another estate agent was taken over by a financial institution. What the financial institution did not realize and what the principals of the estate agency certainly did, was that the property market was starting to tumble.

7 Seller intends to set up a similar operation in competition and take back most, if not all of his customers.

> An office equipment supplier had an agreement drawn up preventing the seller of the acquired company from starting up in a similar business within five years. However, by the end of the second month after the sale was complete, the seller had set up another operation under his wife and top salesman. As he maintained a discreet distance his new business captured nearly all of his old, sold company's customers. Within nine months the acquired business had been closed down by the purchasers and their remaining customers serviced from a unit over two hundred miles away.

8 Market about to be challenged by new or invigorated competitors. Perhaps one of the competitors has just been taken over by a hungry company like yourself.

9 You buy a bad apple along with the business. It is possible, if you are not careful, that there may be someone who will make it their job to spread doom and gloom amongst not only their colleagues, but also your existing staff. You may be buying the very reason the acquired company is not doing as well as it should.

10 Skeletons in the cupboard.

> A small manufacturer took over another manufacturer in the same line of business. The sale stretched the resources of the small company but it just managed to find the cash. Imagine their horror when they found that many customers had had their cheques cashed but no goods supplied, and many suppliers had had bounced cheques that had not been repaid but were down on the books as paid. These problems very nearly brought the small manufacturer down. It survived, however, but £12,000 worse off.

Success criteria

You may well be feeling that acquisition is not for you given all these problems. However, it does remain one of the quickest ways of expanding your business. If you try and guard against all the pitfalls that have been indentified and the others that only experience will bring to you, then you should have a reasonable chance of being really happy with your acquisition. The following is drawn from recent research on successful acquisitions. You might find it useful.

The closer the target business matches these criteria the more successful the acquisition is likely to be:

1 A well-defined market niche.
2 A growing industry.
3 Insensitive to any business cycles.
4 Seasonal stability.
5 Essential products or services – avoid fads or fashions.
6 High added value.
7 Technical know-how.
8 Short production cycle – allows flexibility.
9 Link to the acquirer – should be some relationship in the areas of supplies, production, or sales.
10 Proximity – reduces control problems.

Action

1 Using fig. 7.1, decide what type of company you want to acquire.
2 Find at least three suitable companies and, using fig. 7.2 as a basis, devise a grid to rate their suitability and help you select one to pursue.
3 Set out a clear plan of action. Start off with one the length of an A4 page and develop it from there.

8 Licensing in and buying a franchise

Aims of this chapter

- To introduce the concept of licensing in and explain how to go about it
- To show when licensing in should be used
- To differentiate between licensing and franchising
- To help you go about obtaining a franchise

The concept

Developing your own new product, service or process is an expensive and risky process. On the other hand, acquiring another company that already has a new product, service or process, can be a lot of effort and involve management and negotiating skills that you may feel are not your strong points. Licensing in and franchising provide a kind of 'half-way house'. Both procedures allow you to acquire the product, service, process or even business concept of another organization without going the whole hog and acquiring the organization. The providing organization expects from you, in return, an initial fee and then royalties on sales to:

1 Use its process to produce your goods more effectively.
2 Produce and market its product in markets that they are not serving to any significant extent.
3 Provide its service to a group of organizations or individuals that they are not serving to any great extent.
4 Carry out the same business to new groups of companies or individuals not already served by them.

Clearly you are taking advantage of the research and development of somebody else, and paying them a fee based on sales in return. In situations one, two and three there will be some form of licence agreement and these can be called licensing in opportunities. The fourth situation is a franchise as you are given the entire business concept to run yourself (Tie Rack is a good example of a franchise).

Licensing in

You may well be licensing in at the moment. For instance, much of the software on your computer will be provided under a licence agreement from the originators of the programme. However, if you are to use licensing in as a means of expanding your business, you will have to concentrate on the licensing in opportunities that will significantly alter your turnover or profitability.

It has to be said that most licensing in is the result of chance connection or contact by the owner-manager of the company. Often he or she sees a product or process at a trade show and is immediately hit by the potential of it. Very quickly thereafter a deal is struck and the company is often saddled with something that both fails to maximize the potential of the company and does not easily fit with its existing operation. The results of some licensing in arrangements are therefore disappointing to both sides as its lack of relevance to the company begins to show itself.

Those licensing in agreements that do work are more a function of happy chance than any grand plan. Hence licensing in as a growth strategy needs to be:

  a substantial, so that it does significantly alter the growth rate of the company
  b right, in that it takes account of the strengths of the company and the opportunities in the market place
  c planned, in that it is the result of a strategic decision rather than the outcome of a chance event. This is not to rule out the role of the chance event, but to make sure that such opportunities are taken on only if they move you in the direction you want to go in

A management training organization noticed that their clients were increasingly asking them to make assessments of staff for various leadership characteristics. They made the strategic decision to move into psychological testing as a growth opportunity. As the development of their own testing system would take a lot of time and money to develop, they decided to look at existing systems with the hope of finding one that they could licence. After reviewing several companies they selected the one that appeared to fit their circumstances most exactly. They were then able to enter negotiation with this company secure in the knowledge that it was strategically the correct choice.

How to go about licensing in

The process for going about licensing in involves the following steps:

  1 Decide what you want to build on.
  2 Decide what you are looking for.
  3 Search for possibilities.

4 Decide on those companies you want to approach and select your target.

5 Negotiate the deal.

1 Decide what you want to build on. It is assumed that you have already carried out a SWOT analysis for your firm and you should want to build on the strengths of the firm and take advantage of any opportunities that the analysis has identified. Whatever you do decide to build on must take you towards your aspirations for your company. You can build on:

a Market opportunities. As in the management training example, you may be aware of some opportunity in the market place that would cost you too much in terms of research and development to enter. However, you believe that someone else may already have the solution and be willing, if approached, to let you use it. This may well be an existing product that is offered by the company as a licence opportunity and your task will be to see what is the best version available. Or it may be that the product is produced by someone who has never considered licensing. Here you will be involved in convincing the company that it is in their interests to let you produce the product as well. This is normally acceptable if the company with the product has no expertise in your field of operation or if they are geographically remote from you and have no intentions of entering your area, at least in the foreseeable future. This is more likely to be the case for an overseas manufacturer who is still trying to maximize the potential of their home market (for example, an American manufacturer).

b Existing marketing channels. Your strengths may lie in your salesforce or your distribution system. Perhaps these channels could be used for other products. You may wish to carry out some research to see what opportunities exist in your markets, or you may prefer to see if a search for licensing opportunities leads you to recognize an opportunity. In this situation your search is for something compatible with your marketing channels but you have no specific product in mind.

> Dron and Dickson, who supply and install lighting for hazardous areas such as oil rigs and chemical plants, recognized that generic growth was not necessarily going to provide all the expansion opportunities that its owner, Arthur Rolley, wanted. Therefore, he started looking about for a product that he could sell alongside his existing range of lighting, but which was significantly different from it. He eventually found a Canadian company who were producing a special light that could be placed in a position remote from the area requiring illumination, with the light being transmitted to the required area by means of a reflective pipe. Arthur Rolley immediately saw

the opportunity for this product in the North Sea and the Channel Tunnel, so he negotiated initially to act as European agent for the Canadian company and eventually for a licence agreement to manufacture the product in the UK.

c The production process. You may feel that there ought to be better ways of producing your products than you are doing at present. A close examination of the production process, perhaps using the government's Manufacturing Initiative, will probably show up some areas for improvement, or certain operations that could be automated.

> AM Graphics recognized that the proofing system that they used to help clients see what a colour leaflet or poster would look like before it was printed, was not of the same standard as that of the big printing and reprographic firms.Whilst they considered trying to compete with the big firms and bring in an expensive colour proofing system, they looked around for other processes. Andie Thompson, the owner of AM Graphics, was delighted when he found an alternative new process that he could get, under licence, considerably more cheaply, but that gave as good a result as the existing systems.

d Existing underutilized resources. It may be that your workforce is highly skilled and you don't want to lose them but equally you don't have the work to occupy them full time. You may have spare capacity in your production process or room in your premises.

2 Decide what you are looking for. Once you have decided the area it is often the case that what you are looking for becomes perfectly obvious. As in the AM Graphics example, it was clear that a production process was required in a clearly defined area. However in the Dron and Dickson example, all Arthur Rolley started off with was his existing sales operation. He then had to decide whether he should be looking within the lighting industry or further afield. And if further afield, then which area should it be.

3 Search for possibilities. This can be divided into those search strategies that involve reacting to companies that are looking for licensing partners, and those strategies where you search for licence opportunities with companies that have not so far considered the idea. The first group can be seen as reactive strategies, the second group as proactive strategies.

a Reactive strategies. There are several areas where you can search for other companies who might be interested in licensing arrangements:

Foreign consulates. They often produce lists or publications of those companies in their country who are looking to licence their product or process into the UK. You can ask to be put on their mailing list or take it further and talk to the commercial attaché and explain and specify the type of thing you are looking for. The British Overseas Trade Board (BOTB) collates a lot of this information from Embassies and Consulates in the UK and publishes it regularly. Further information is available from:

The British Overseas Trade Board, 1-19 Victoria St, London SW1H 0ET. Tel : 01 215 7877.

Trade magazines. Whilst occasionally you will find companies advertising for licensing partners, trade magazines are more useful for articles on those companies wishing to expand and looking for partners to manufacture under licence. It is also useful to 'phone the editorial staff on the magazine and ask them if they know of any companies who are looking for licensing partners.

Trade shows. These are a great source of intelligence. By asking around and visiting all the stands you can soon find out who is thinking of licensing out their product or process.

b Proactive strategies. These searches can be made within a particular industry, as in the one you have selected as the target, or they can be within a particular technology, assuming that it is a process that you are after, or occasionally, within a geographic area, such as the USA.

Trade shows. You can use these to assess the products or technologies that you would like to get hold of, and research the various different companies with something to offer.

Trade magazines. Many trade magazines have an innovations column and this can be a rich source of opportunities. Some newspapers too, *The Financial Times* and *The Sunday Times,* have special columns on innovations.

Trade registers. For example, *Thomas's Register for America,* contains a huge number of US firms advertising their products or services. It is like a combination of *Yellow Pages* and a *Kompass* directory in that it lists companies by industrial sector with a fair amount of description about each company's products.

A word of caution concerning searching for licences. If your research consists of writing 'cold' to potential licensors you must make sure that your methods are more personalized. You and they need to be very clear why you are contacting them and what you are offering or hoping for. You will then have a greater chance of obtaining replys from the sort of companies you would be particularly interested in.

New Enterprise Development decided to select certain product types, from *Thomas's Register for America* for which they felt there would be a market in the UK. They then sent duplicate, 'standard' letters to all the companies in

Thomas's that looked good bets, offering to manufacture, under licence, their product in Europe. However, this produced a fairly disappointing response, and those that did reply were generally not the sort of companies that the company would want to deal with.

4 Decide on those companies you want to approach and select your target. When making a decision about the company you are hoping to do business with, you should consider the following indicators:

a Their standing within their industry. You will normally find this out by 'phoning some other companies in their industry and discussing with them their views on the subject.

b Their financial viability. This can be found out from their accounts or some idea achieved through your bank contacting their bank. You could also use a credit rating company like Dunn and Bradstreet to give you a detailed financial assessment of the company. This may cost you up to £100 for each company.

c Their age. You may feel that the more established the firm the more secure will be your proposed licence agreement. The company's age can normally be found out simply by 'phoning their telephonist or receptionist and asking them.

d Suppliers' references. As you narrow your choice down to one or two target companies, it is worth talking to their suppliers to get some idea of their standing with them.

e Product/process quality. Again this is probably best researched through asking others in their industry.

5 Negotiate the deal. You will want firm answers or agreements on:

a Royalties. The downpayment fee and the ongoing royalty that you will pay to them for selling their product or using their process. This will normally be a fairly large lump sum at the start and a small percentage (normally between five per cent and ten per cent of sales) on each sale.

b Payments. The timing of any licence agreement payments. You want these to be as long after you have sold the product as you can get, and paid at regular times, like quarterly in arrears.

c Market place. The territory you will be able to operate in. This is normally to ensure that separate licensees don't overlap as far as selling territories are concerned. You will want this to be as large as possible but with as little in the way of guaranteed minimum sales to achieve in a given time span as possible.

d Help. How much technical help you are going to get from them when you start. You want as much as you can get at as little cost to you as possible (remember, if you don't ask you probably won't get).

e Suppliers. Who will be the suppliers? You will probably obtain any source components or subassemblies from the licensor initially but you will want leeway to obtain your sources independently if and when you want to. Equally you will want to know if local suppliers provide materials of the standard required and charge prices that are reasonable and of the going rate.

f Quality. What quality standards will be expected. Will these be too high for you to produce things economically?

g Termination. How you will end the agreement. It is always advisable to work out your escape route before you venture into the fray.

Licensing in holds many opportunities to get started in a product area by climbing onto the shoulders of someone who has gone through all the problems and frustrations of the research and development stage. Provided you stick to licences that are with companies of some standing and you play to your existing strengths and opportunities, then licensing in can offer a low-risk route to fairly swift growth.

Legal structure

Get your lawyer involved at an early stage and try to ensure that the agreement is drawn up under UK law, unless you are an expert in the law of the country of origin of the licensor.

Buying a franchise

This is very similar to licensing in except that the whole business system is under licence to you rather than just a particular product, process or service. A franchise will normally include:

a the product or service
b the selling process
c the image and design
d the store layout and furnishings (if it is a retail outlet)
e the raw materials
f the accounting system
g the training system

In fact it includes virtually everything you need to run that business. The franchisor may even arrange loans for you to pay for the business.

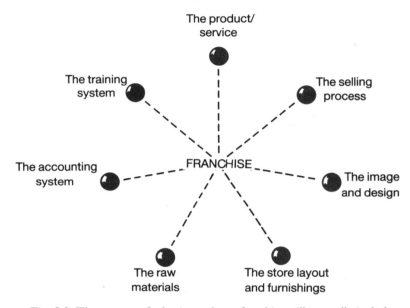

Fig. 8.1 The aspects of a business that a franchise will normally include

Finding a suitable franchise

There are more and more franchise exhibitions being held where you can view many different opportunities and compare costs and benefits. It is also worth subscribing to one of the franchise publications, such as *The Franchise Magazine* or *Franchise World*, available from their respective addresses:

The Franchise Magazine, Franchise Development Services, Castle House, Castle Meadow, Norwich NR2 1PJ. Tel: 0603 620301.

Franchise World, Franchise Publications, Jones House, 37 Nottingham Rd, London SW17 7EA. Tel: 01 767 1371.

The British Franchise Association can give you a lot of advice and information on franchising and if a franchisor is a member of the Association you can be fairly confident of the quality of the business he is offering. Their address is:

The British Franchise Association, 75a Bell St, Henley-on-Thames RG9 2BD. Tel: 0491 578049/50.

Fig. 8.2 Franchise publications
Courtesy: *Franchise World*

Also *Exchange and Mart* has a section on business opportunities in which there appear a number of franchise offers.

Assessing a franchise opportunity

The British Franchise Association can provide you with a checklist to assess franchises, but here are a few pointers:

1 How long have they being trading? (at least more than two years to be more confident)
2 Will they show you their accounts, both total and for individual outlets?
3 Are they professional? (in approach, literature, product, and so on)
4 Talk to a few of their existing franchisees and find out what the franchise is worth.
5 How much are they asking in terms of fee plus royalty against projected and actual profits?
6 How much will you be expected to pay?
7 How detailed is their business plan?
8 What is the market like for their product or service?
9 Is the market growing?
10 How many competitors are there?
11 How many franchises have they sold already? (the more the better, although getting in early is certainly cheaper but much more risky)
12 Does their franchise look professional?
13 Are the franchisors and existing franchisees your sort of people?

Taking the plunge

It is important to get your lawyer involved. Do not sign anything until you are absolutely clear what you are signing and have done your homework on the company and the business plan for the franchise. Also do some market research to test reaction to the concept in your area or amongst your existing clients.

Clearly, as this is a 'complete' business, it has to be operated separately to your existing operation and this may give you administrative and personnel problems. Watch that you do not stretch yourself too far. Try to choose a franchise that fits in well with your existing business and your capabilities.

Action

1 Decide what area of your business you feel you could take advantage of with a licence agreement. Is it:
  a sales channels
  b underutilized staff
  c addition to the product or service offering
  d underutilized resources
  e market opportunity?
2 Decide what you are looking for and draw up a search strategy on one side of A4 paper.
3 Draw up some assessment criteria to evaluate the various licensing opportunities you discover.
4 Draw up a one page plan of action as to how you will integrate the new product, process or service into your business.
5 Decide on your bottom line in negotiations based on a quick calculation of the trading budget of the licence opportunity.
6 Decide what type of franchise will most suit your capabilities and resources.
7 Draw up a franchise search strategy on one side of A4 paper.
8 Decide how you will evaluate each franchise opportunity.
9 Set out an action plan on one side of A4 paper.
10 Do it!

9 Joint ventures and strategic alliances

Aims of this chapter

- To explain what joint ventures are and how they might be helpful to you in developing a project that your business alone cannot undertake

- To show that even the smallest of companies can benefit from a joint venture

- To point out the pitfalls of joint ventures and to explain how to go about avoiding them

- To explain the differences between joint ventures and strategic alliances and to show that many companies often indulge in strategic alliances without actually realizing it

- To help you get the best out of a strategic alliance and to assess when it is an appropriate means of taking advantage of an opportunity

Joint ventures

Joint ventures are where two companies decide to form a third company that they both own. This new company takes resources from both its 'parents' to exploit an opportunity that both the parents were aware of but could not take advantage of on their own. It is often a fifty-fifty relationship although shareholdings can vary a lot between the two partners.

Why do they come about?

Essentially, joint ventures come about through two companies working together in an area and discovering an opportunity that neither can handle on their own. The companies may already have a close relationship, either through working in a related field, such as supplier and customer, or by being one of a network of companies which have personal contacts with an owner-manager who is looking to expand his business.

The reasons for considering this option are:

1 Size of project. The project is too big for the initiator party to handle on their own.

> Liquid Levers considered a joint venture for one of their inventions because they could not raise the finance themselves. They decided to approach those companies that not only had the financial clout but also had a strong presence in selling and distribution in the area of their new product.

2 Risk. The project is too risky for either party to handle on their own.

3 Lack of expertise. Neither party has all the capabilities and expertise to make a success of the project.

> AM Graphics formed a joint venture with an advertising agency client of theirs to take advantage of the lack of a local advertising agency in AM Graphics' area. This benefited them both because previously the advertising agency were unable to move into the area as it was geographically remote from them and they had no contacts; and AM could not take advantage of the opportunity because the media would not give them credit or commission as they did not qualify as a recognized advertising agency.

4 Image. The new project does not fit with either party's current image in the market place.

5 Control. Neither party wants to give up total control.

6 Trial period for acquisition purposes. It can provide a 'toe in the water' approach to finding out about potential acquisition prior to making the final move. As discussed in Chapter 7, acquisition is a very risky area because of two dissimilar cultures coming together. A joint venture can help the acquiring company determine if an acquisition will work by using the joint venture to observe the other company at much closer quarters.

7 Defence against an unwelcome takeover. Some family firms start getting into problems as shares get more widely dispersed through events such as deaths, births, and marriages. It can be the case that more than 50 per cent of the shares are held by people who have no interest in the firm. By negotiating a joint venture agreement with a friendly firm, it is possible to write into the agreement that the friendly firm has first option to buy the family firm in the case of a takeover attempt.

8 Overcoming a company's deficiencies. Joint ventures can be created by one party seeking out a partner to compensate for their deficiencies.

Posta Print found that although their idea to produce a new type of postcard was enthusiastically received by potential customers and the trade, they could not get it properly off the ground because they lacked a distribution and marketing operation. After researching various card and postcard distributors they found a company that not only could market the product but could also solve some reproduction problems Posta Print were having. It was decided that the most appropriate vehicle to proceed with was a joint venture.

Joint ventures will look very attractive to your expansion plans because they look as if they avoid a lot of the headaches associated with other approaches to expansion. This is because they appear to:

a spread the risk
b reduce the cost
c distance the risk into a separate company
d take advantage of the strengths and experience of both parties whilst minimizing their weaknesses
e get around the barriers faced by an individual company
f take advantage of an opportunity that otherwise would fall to someone else
g sometimes build on an existing relationship to the mutual benefit of both parties

However, all the research into this form of business expansion suggests that it has a surprisingly low success rate: slightly less than 50 per cent. Why should this be so? There are a number of explanations for this and these are worth bearing in mind when considering this option for expanding your business.

1 It is riskier to move into an area in which you only have partial knowledge and experience.
2 Frequently the management of the new company is unclear since both parents have their own ideas as to how it should be run. Indeed the management of the joint third company will also probably have further ideas and views.
3 Just like marriage, people's needs change, and what is important to your company just now may well not be what is important to it in the future. You may well not devote all the necessary attention and resources that are required to ensure the success of the joint venture.
4 Joint venturing is like diversification without the same control for both companies. As already seen, it is difficult enough when one company diversifies, without having both companies having to feel their way around.
5 It is, after all, a start-up of a new company with all the

dangers that this entails. There are new structures and organizational problems that are unique to a new enterprise and which are the source of many problems that can eventually lead to the demise of the venture.

6 It is a costly thing to set up, involving, as it does, a new corporate structure and all the negotiations and legal arrangements that are required to keep both parties happy.

Thus to be successful, a joint venture has to:

a fulfil a need of both companies
b be managed by only one or preferably neither of the partners
c fulfil a significant opportunity in the market
d make maximum use of the strengths of either party and minimalize the reliance on areas of weakness in either party
e benefit both parties to a significant degree
f be between people that enjoy working with each other and respect what the other is bringing to the venture (a meeting of minds and personalities)

How to go about it

This will be examined in two sections reflecting the two main situations by which you can go about setting up a joint venture.

Situation 1. This situation is where you recognize an opportunity but you cannot take advantage of it yourself, either because you don't have the resources or experience or because you feel that you are not geared up to cope with it as well as you could do with the help of someone else. This is similar to the licensing in problem discussed in the last chapter, only here you are clear at the start what you require in the way of help, so you have some idea of the profile of your target company already. Look at the whole project and assess which areas you are strong in and which areas show up weaknesses. Draw up a grid like the one opposite.

By completing fig. 9.1 you can obtain a clear picture of the areas that you need help in and hence the profile of the company you should look to as a potential partner.

Your search will involve all the areas suggested for licensing in but as the target company may well be in an industry with which you are not familiar, it is useful to use as many of your contacts to help you as you can. The route that takes you to a potential partner is sometimes quite bizarre.

The wife of an owner-manager who had a project that he could not handle himself, attended an export seminar at which she talked to the managing director of another firm that she had just met that day. They happened to touch on the problem but no more than that. The managing director was

Aspects of the project:	Very strong	Fairly strong	So-so	Fairly weak	Very weak
Development					
Production					
Finance					
Market knowledge					
Sales expertise					
Distribution					
Influence suppliers					
Promotion					
Image					

Fig. 9.1 Assessing your strengths and weaknesses in your new project

having lunch a few day later with the European production director of an American multinational who happened to mention that they were looking for new ideas. The managing director remembered the conversation he had had at the export seminar and later that day contacted the owner-manager's wife and asked if it would be in order for him to mention to this multinational their idea. She agreed and although the negotiations eventually fell through, the company then had a much clearer idea of the type of company they wanted and contacted similar organizations to the American multinational, soon effecting an agreement.

Once you have found a suitable candidate you must satisfy yourself that they are the right one by evaluating them in the same way as you would a licensor. However, you will also want to bear in mind the factors that go to make a successful joint venture that were discussed earlier in this chapter.

Once you are in a position to start negotiations it is essential that you involve your advisors. However, make sure that they are expert in joint venture agreements. There is nothing worse than relying on your firm of accountants of many years if they have never been involved in negotiating a joint venture. There are also many consultants who claim expertise in this area and who offer you help at a cost. Again make sure of their credentials to handle this type of situation by talking to others who have used them.

Situation 2. This second situation deals with those joint ventures that arise out of a close working relationship with a customer, supplier, advisor, or colleague company in your industry.

Here there is no need to search for a partner since the partner already exists. Evaluation is also much easier since you know so much more about your potential partner. However, you may find it useful to complete fig. 9.1 for both organizations to make sure that all aspects of the project are well covered and that there are no glaring gaps.

It is when it comes to negotiation that it can get more complicated than the first situation. There can often be more at stake: existing friendships or existing custom. It is therefore advisable in these circumstances to leave as much as possible to the advisors with the broad thrust of the agreement having been decided between the parties beforehand.

Strategic alliances

A strategic alliance is a much less complex method of tackling a project with a partner than a joint venture. It involves simply an agreement, which is often just verbal, to tackle a particular situation together with another company.

Many companies are already using this method to expand their businesses without realizing that they are forming a strategic alliance.

> TMS Advertising and Arthur Young, the accountants, got together to tackle the tourism development market. TMS had, for a number of years, built up an expertise in tourism marketing dealing with individual operators, regional tourist boards and the Scottish Tourist Board. When two top executives from the Scottish Tourist Board joined Arthur Young's tourism development unit, a link was created between the two organizations. After some discussions, TMS and Arthur Young decided that they would like to offer a package that involved both development and marketing to tourist organizations. This joint package was given a name and a joint brochure was produced. The subsequent work that resulted was divided between the two organizations according to their expertise. This arrangement proved very successful, and without having to form a separate company. TMS and Arthur Young had formed a strategic alliance to handle this market opportunity.

The basic ingredients for a strategic alliance are the same as for a joint venture, but without the in-depth analysis that a joint venture requires.

The advantages of a strategic alliance are:

1 It is not a new start so you avoid the structural and organizational problems that such a structure entails.
2 It is simpler because no new legal identity is created.
3 It is a faster route into the market than a joint venture which

can take over a year to complete.

4 It is easier to disentangle if something goes wrong.

5 It is less costly to set up.

So, why bother with a joint venture? There are many situations where you wish to distance yourself from the effects of the project by having it as a separate company. It is also important because it is a legal structure and does protect the participants in a way that even the best drawn up legal agreement to cooperate does not. Strategic alliances may well be the precursor in some cases to joint ventures, especially if the project becomes very successful and its sheer size dictates that it might be more efficiently handled as a separate company.

The disadvantages of a strategic alliance are:

1 You would be well advised to draw up some form of legal agreement as companies have found themselves getting little or no money from the agreement if the partner collects all the invoices.

2 You may well be left holding the baby if your partner disowns the alliance or goes bust.

3 You may well set up a market for your partner that they exploit without giving you any share of it.

Strategic alliances are an increasingly popular way of tackling particular market opportunities, and with a little bit of care they can afford considerable growth potential in markets that you would normally not be able to tackle.

One final, important point. When drawing up a legal agreement in a strategic alliance or a company in a joint venture, insist that it is drawn up under UK law. Otherwise, if anything goes wrong, it will cost you a great deal of money and time carrying out litigation under a foreign legal system.

Action

1 If there is a project that you want to pursue but cannot because of a lack of resources or experience, see if there is another company that might help you get it off the ground.

2 By assessing the risk and the investment involved decide whether a joint venture or strategic alliance would be better.

3 Try to find more than one candidate for your partner and assess them according to how much they compliment your skills, resources, experience, and so on.

4 Don't join up with someone unless you are 100 per cent happy about the deal.

10 Licensing out and franchising

Aims of this chapter

- To help you understand what licensing out is and to differentiate between licensing to *enter* a market (market entry licensing) and licensing to *develop* a market (market development licensing)
- To develop a system for finding the right licensing partner(s)
- To point out the dangers and advantages of licensing
- To help you see how franchising can give your company rapid growth
- To point out the likely pitfalls of expanding through franchising

Licensing out

Licensing out occurs when a small firm decides to give their product or process to other firms in return for a fee based on the number of products sold or the amount of use of the process.

Why license out?

1 **Enables fast growth**. It allows very fast growth in sales of a product without the hassle of producing it, financing it or selling it. Obviously it is only your royalty payment that goes into your profit and loss account, but for this you have only very minor costs involved. It is therefore a means of increasing the profitability of the company rather than a means of increasing the turnover dramatically.

2 **Provides 'free' money**. The revenue from licence fees is virtually free money for the small business as it involves little or no expense and comes in on a regular basis from the licensee. This allows an innovative small firm, for example, Liquid Levers, to concentrate on research and development being sure in the knowledge that revenue is coming in without having to generate sales. There are many small firms who passionately believe that they should retain complete control of their innovation. These firms rarely have the financial resources to develop through generic

growth and as already seen it is a very slow process. Licensing out is a golden opportunity to develop your firm and see mass production and purchase of your idea without having to go through the trauma of generic growth.

3 Builds market share. By licensing out your product you can quite quickly build up a strong market share which will allow you and your licensees to dominate the market and begin to take advantage of the price determination that this allows. The more market share you have for a product the greater the chance you have of getting a decent price. Your promotional costs become a much smaller part of the cost of each product the better known it gets through its greater exposure in the market place. Your licensees are paying for part or perhaps all of your promotional costs.

4 Provides resources. It allows projects to go ahead that would normally fail because of the lack of resources of the small firm. For example, one of Liquid Levers products, its truck tyre sensor, was licensed out, simply because the development and marketing costs were too vast for the company to consider. It did not have the financial standing to attract sufficient funds such that they could retain control of their firm so they opted for the licensing out route.

5 Enter new markets quickly. By licensing your product to companies in different markets to yourself you can diversify into new markets without the risk that is normally associated with such a move. Indeed, it is possible to achieve virtual worldwide distribution of your product in a very short space of time using your licensing agreements. It would be impossible to do this under your own resources in anything like same timescale.

6 Builds market awareness. It helps build a market awareness that could prevent others from copying your idea. Often small businesses try to launch their new idea themselves but frequently with insufficient capital. Others see the idea, copy it, and because of better resources, dominate the market before you have had time to establish yourself.

7 Spreads costs of development. This often happens where the small firm seeks the assistance of a larger firm to distribute its product. For example, Liquid Levers' truck tyre sensor is being partially developed by its licensee.

How to go about it

There are companies who specialize in helping with licensing. Details are available from:

However it is useful to gain an understanding of the best ways of going about licensing out. Again a basic model is used:

1 Decide the type of company you are aiming at.
2 Search for the right companies.
3 Select the ones you wish to pursue.
4 Decide the licensing plan you want.
5 Negotiate.
6 Monitor what goes on.
7 Involve and inform your licensee(s).

1 Decide the type of company you are aiming at. There are two ways of looking at this. Either you are looking for a big company to help you get into the market (market entry licensing), or you are trying to get a number of companies to take on your product or service to build your market share (market development licensing). With market entry licensing, you are looking for a company that can cope with virtually everything from final development to production and marketing. With market development licensing you are generally looking for smaller companies who can add your product or service to their existing range with the minimum of extra cost or change in their sales and promotion procedures. Whatever the process you will want to develop a profile of the most likely type of company as a basis for your search. You will find it useful to create a thumbnail sketch of the type of company you are looking for. For example:

'Our target company is British owned with some overseas connections in the Middle East. It has a turnover of £5 million and has been trading for twenty years. It has a BS 5750 system of quality control and subcontracts most of its subassembly work. It has a large salesforce who deal direct with our target market and it has complementary products to ours.'

The chances of finding just such a company are remote, but it helps make more vivid the type of company that you are looking for.

2 Search for the right companies. If you are pursuing market entry licensing you will find that the process is similar to that for finding the right company for a joint venture (see previous chapter). However, if you are interested in market development licensing then you will tend to use the following channels:

a trade shows
b trade press
c British Overseas Trade Board (BOTB) if you want to license overseas
d national newspapers, particularly *The Financial Times*
e your personal network of contacts
f suppliers
g trade organizations
h chambers of commerce
i local authority economic development departments

3 Select the ones you wish to pursue. If you are market entry licensing, this will involve the in-depth analysis that was described in the joint venture chapter. If you are licensing to develop your share then you will find it useful to employ a rating system somewhat like fig. 10.1. You list a number of attributes that your ideal companies should have and possibly weight them in terms of importance. (The weights shown in fig. 10.1 are just an example. You should determine your own weights or decide to weight all attributes the same.) Then you rate each potential company out of ten for each attribute. The total figure can be very useful in helping you to decide whether to take on each company that is interested in pursuing your licensing offer.

Attribute	Weight	Company rating
Customer base	1.5	
Financial stability	1.3	
Production capability	0.7	
Image	0.3	
Their staff	0.8	
Their sales projection	1.0	
Location	0.6	
Suppliers	0.4	
Quality control	1.3	
Fit with existing products	1.2	
		Total:

Fig. 10.1 Selecting your company

4 Decide the licensing plan you want. To a certain extent this has to be tempered by what the market will bear. However, it is normal to look for some form of up-front payment and then a royalty of between 6 and 10 per cent of sales. You will need to decide how you want this paid. It is often done on an annual basis, but you may wish to start off with monthly payments until you get confidence in the licensee. You will need cast iron clauses to prevent further production of your product if the licensee fails to hit certain targets. And you will want to decide what a reasonable target for sales is. Remember that you can always word your agreement to give you the option to take action but this doesn't mean that you have to take it if you feel the company is having genuine problems.

5 Negotiate. If you haven't done much negotiating before it is worth reading about it. Gavin Kennedy's *Everything is Negotiable* is very helpful and good fun to read. You are well advised to involve your professional advisors at this point, as it often helps that after you and the prospective licensee have agreed the broad outline of the deal they can be left to sort out the small print. This helps prevent your relationship with the licensee becoming soured over some small point which is nevertheless important but can be sorted out at another level by professionals (remember, do make sure that legal documents are drawn up under UK laws). If you are licensing out for market development, then you will take a more inflexible approach at this stage, only really altering what you want if you find it hard to get any takers or you feel you are getting licensees too easily. Remember: it is essential that both sides in the negotiation feel that they have a good deal. If your licensees feel they have been taken for a ride then you can be sure that they will try everything to redress the balance during their period of manufacture and selling of the product.

6 Monitor what goes on. While your agreement will have stated how you will determine sales figures (normally licensees must make their books available at any time and any dispute is arbitrated by an independent accountant) it is useful to keep a close check on the sales figures to see if they are going according to plan so that corrective action can be taken immediately. It is also a good idea to keep up the development of the product yourself. This gives licensees confidence that they are not going to be left behind with an out of date product in a year or two, and convinces them that you are not licensing out simply in order to gain a quick profit.

7 Involve and inform your licensee(s). It is a good idea to try to involve your licensees in developing the product themselves. This reduces your costs but you still get the benefit if you word your agreement to your advantage but not to their disadvantage. Also keep your licensees informed of what is happening with the product and with other licensees. Keep closely in touch with them to pick up any problems early on and to encourage and motivate them to greater efforts.

Problems

Inevitably there can be problems with this form of expansion. It is worth looking out for the following situations:

1 The licensee's managing director is not behind the project. If this is the case, there is every likelihood that the licensee will not live up to expectations and the agreement terminated.
2 You issue too many licences and can't keep control of them. This often results in poorly motivated licensees and frequent quality problems.
3 Licensees are not committed to the project because they want the licence for another reason. This may simply be to stop your product damaging the sales of their product that yours puts out of date. It may be for other obscure reasons connected with their competitors.
4 Taking too long to consummate the deal. If you are licensing for market entry then it is typical for negotiations to take a very long time. Watch that you don't become totally dependent on the outcome being successful. Put a very definite timescale on each stage of your negotiations and withdraw if your potential licensees are dragging things out. If they are really serious they will very quickly get round any problems they have at the negotiation stage. You might only have to approach another potential licensee for awkward companies to change their attitude completely and try much harder to get the licence. If you don't work this way it is quite possible for your eye to be taken off your existing business for so long that it becomes severely damaged.
5 Keep a very strict quality control. If you don't, then it is your reputation that is being harmed and the continued success of all your licence agreements on this product and possibly others. That is why it is so important to keep the number of licences to a level that you can monitor effectively and keep the quality up.

Licensing out for market development is a very quick way of expanding your business provided you have something that other companies want. So if you want to indulge in this form of

Fig. 10.2 Examples of the help available for your licensing out and/or franchising strategy

expansion, make sure you are constantly on the lookout for new ideas to keep you ahead of the field and able to offer something that others want. You may even need to protect the idea with a patent or copyright. You will probably want to contact a patent agent to help you in this. Names and addresses of ones in your area are available from:

The Chartered Institute of Patent Agents, Staple Inn Buildings, High Holborn, London WC1V 7PZ. Tel: 01 405 9450.

Franchising

With the success of The Body Shop and the advent of McDonald's, franchising is very much to the fore as a means of getting into business. However, it is also a very useful and obvious way of expanding your business.

What is franchising?

Franchising is very similar to licensing out but instead of licensing a product or process you license the entire business concept. The prospective franchisee pays you a sum of money to buy your business concept. He or she will also pay a royalty on sales and be constrained to sell only what you allow and which will normally be supplied by you. You will also provide the corporate identity, packaging and layout and design of the store if it is a retail operation. The reason why the franchisee is so keen to subjugate himself to this situation is that you have a proven workable idea and the failure rate of franchises is much lower than standard businesses. Indeed, it is generally regarded that if you can secure a McDonald's franchise then you are virtually guaranteed to become a millionaire within five years (although even some McDonald's franchises have been known to fail).

How do you franchise your operation?

You have to have something that is franchiseable and that means it is a self-contained operation that can be relatively quickly set up and can exist within a certain territory. Criteria include:

1 You have to have a well-established operation with at least two successful years of trading accounts.
2 Your business must be financially sound before you give any thought to franchising the operation. It takes a lot of money to launch a franchise operation properly. There is, for instance, all the promotional literature, sales meetings and legal matters to fund.

3 The business is simple or easily communicated to prospective franchisees as they have to grasp the essence of it quickly to be encouraged to investigate it further.
4 It has to be transferable. It is no good if it only works for you because of the attributes of your area, for example, the availability of particular raw materials or the make-up of your customers. You have to make sure of this transferability aspect otherwise you'll end up with an irate franchisee threatening to sue you for tricking him into buying a worthless franchise.
5 You need to have developed a strong brand image that is established in the market place. For example, Tie Rack was particularly good at doing everything they could to maximize public awareness about their operation in order to establish the brand and therefore make the selling of franchises all the more easy.
6 You need to make sure that you have all the necessary trade mark, design copyright and patent protection that you need. If you don't, it will not be the first time that a prospective franchisor has been ready to launch only to find that some quick-thinking entrepreneur has registered the name and trade mark in the franchisor's primary export market.
7 You will need to be capable of motivating your franchisees as this is a fundamental aspect of franchising. For example, every year Apollo Blinds hires a huge hall for all its franchisees and provides a highly motivational day's conference. You need to keep in contact constantly, especially at the start, to nip in the bud any potential problems and to weed out quickly any unsuitable franchisees before they have had time to do any damage to your image. For instance, McDonald's insists that a prospective franchisee works unpaid in another McDonald's outlet for a year in order to learn the ropes.

Most reputable franchise operations are members of the British Franchise Association. Membership is not easy to come by and you need to get roughly two years of successful franchises up and running before you will stand a chance of getting in. The Association is very helpful if you are thinking of going ahead and they are certainly essential to talk to before going ahead. They can be contacted at:

The British Franchise Association, 75a Bell St, Henley-on-Thames RG9 2BD. Tel: 0491 578049/50.

There are several consultancies (one which is even a franchise operation itself) which have been set up to help companies who wish to franchise their business. They tend to be fairly expensive and you have to be seriously considering franchising before pointing yourself in their direction. Names and addresses are available from the British Franchise Association.

Franchising holds untold potential for the right sort of operation but it can be a very expensive process to set up and monitor. The rewards are high but so are the stakes. It is vital that you keep very strict quality control and motivate like mad. That said it is still the most exciting method of expansion for small business, provided it is suitable.

Action

1 Take a cool, hard look at your business. Is it really going to satisfy your ambitions without letting another company help you?

2 If the answer is no then decide which of the licensing and franchise options would suit your situation.

3 Write down ten things that you need to do to make your idea franchiseable or licenseable.

4 Devise a short plan of action along the lines suggested in this chapter.

5 Put it into action by putting your licence/franchise package together. Start with an A4 sheet outlining:

   a what is the opportunity
   b what is the approximate market
   c what is the process (how do you produce the product or deliver the service)
   d a rough profit/loss calculation
   e what is the proposed deal

6 Start your search now by listing ten people you will contact to develop a list of target companies.

11 Financing expansion

Aims of this chapter

- To show you that there are many sources of finance to choose from
- To explain how each of the funders view your project and to explain what they are looking for in return for their money.
- To help you realize that funders are suppliers and that you need to negotiate the best deal you can with them

In a book dedicated to the strategies of small business expansion, it is not possible to cover in any real depth the issue of financing your expansion. However, this chapter will serve to cover the major areas and to point you in the direction of further help.

Amount of finance required

The amount of money you will require will be determined by your business plan.

Some expansion strategies require very little in the way of finance. These are:

a licensing out
b some strategic alliances
c some franchising

Other expansion strategies require moderate amounts of money often spread over a period of time as they are required to fund cash flow. These are:

a market development
b generic growth
c strategic alliances
d some franchising
e some leveraged buyouts

Quite sizeable amounts of money are required when some sort of investment is needed to get the strategy up and running. This is normally the purchasing of a licence or the funding of moderate research and development. These are:

a diversification
b licensing in
c some product development
d some acquisitions
e franchising

Lastly there are some projects that require very large sums of money, well over £200,000. These are:

a some acquisitions
b some product development
c some diversification

Clearly there are going to be the exceptions to this classification and according to the size and resources of your organization you may view virtually all sums required as very large. However, the size of the sum you require will determine to a fair degree which sources of finance you will need to approach.

Financing your expansion: step by step

Step 1: Assess the requirement

Once you know what you want to do, you will plan it out and create a business plan with an accompanying profit and loss, projected balance sheet, and cash flow. The cash flow will show how much money is required not only for the investment but also for the subsequent working capital. It is easy, for instance, to look only on the price of the purchase of a new piece of machinery as the amount of money required, and fail to also take into account the resulting working capital requirement. Your accountant should be asked to help you prepare these financial statements. But a word of caution: don't let him or her do it all. That way you won't understand what is going on and will be at a distinct disadvantage when it comes to in-depth discussions with potential funders. Make a first stab at it yourself and then get your accountant to check and develop your figures.

Cash flows seem to create a major stumbling block for some small business people. Here are some hints to get you started:

1 Draw up a rough profit/loss for the next year.
2 Split this up into individual months by simply dividing your annual figures by twelve.
3 For your monthly sales projection:
   a alter the figures to take account of any seasonal fluctuations
   b change the figures to take account of the introduction of

your expansion plans and the build-up of sales that will occur (you will not reach your regular sales level from month one)

    c find out how much the monthly sales now add up to and if this differs from your annual projection, alter the figures so that it doesn't, or reassess your annual projection

    d make sure that the monthly figures make sense and adjust where necessary

4 Alter your monthly cost of sales figures to take account of these new monthly sales figures.

5 Adjust your overhead figures to take account of when you would actually be billed for them. In the case of wages, take account of any new staff hired at the time they are hired.

6 Now that you have a monthly profit/loss forecast it is easy to do the cash flow. Table 1 shows the process for sales. Don't forget to include existing debtors (people who owe you money) at the start. Offset the cash according to the number of days on average people take to pay you. (You can make a rough estimate of this by dividing the debtors on the balance sheet from your last set of accounts by the sales in your profit/loss account, and then mulitiplying this by 365 days). For example, if the answer is 45 days, then offset half the month one sales amount by one month, and half by two months and so on.

		Month 1	Month 2	Month 3	Month 4
Monthly sales		£20,000	£30,000	£60,000	£40,000
Debtors	£50,000				
Cash in		£25,000	£35,000	£25,000	£45,000

Table 1

7 Now do the same for cost of sales estimating how long on average you take to pay your suppliers and subcontractors. If your expansion involves new suppliers and subcontractors make sure that you take account of any change in credit arrangements, like initially having to prepay your account until you build up a track record. Table 2 shows this with you paying your suppliers on average after 60 days but with half the cost of sales in month three when the expansion takes place having to be prepaid.

		Month 1	Month 2	Month 3	Month 4
Cost of sales		£10,000	£15,000	£30,000	£20,000
Creditors	£40,000				
Cash out		£20,000	£20,000	£25,000	£15,000

Table 2

8 Now put down when you will have to pay each of your monthly overhead items.

9 By adding up all the cash out items in a month you will have a total cash requirement for that month.

Table 3 shows how this gives rise to your cash required or bank balance.

	Month 1	Month 2	Month 3	Month 4
Cash in	£25,000	£35,000	£25,000	£45,000
Cash out cost of sales	£20,000	£20,000	£25,000	£15,000
Overheads (total payments in that month)	£10,000	£12,000	£20,000	£15,000
Total cash out	£30,000	£32,000	£45,000	£30,000
Net cash in/(out)	(£5000)	£3000	(£20,000)	£15,000
Balance brought forward	£2000	(£3000)	0	(£20,000)
Bank balance	(£3000)	0	(£20,000)	(£5000)

Table 3

10 This is probably your true requirement but it is worth considering if there are any ways that it could be worse, or that you could improve it, to give you three cash flows: a best possible, a worst possible and a most likely.

Step 2: Assess your own resources

Whilst you will probably prefer to get some help with your financial requirements, don't forget that it costs you money. Equally it is worth knowing the bottom line of your requirement should funding prove difficult. Check through this list to build up a picture of your resources:

1 Have you any personal cash that you can invest?

2 How much further could you stretch your creditors before paying them? By initially delaying payment for a number of days at the cash requirement point and then making regular but perhaps not quite full payments for a while thereafter, it is possible to raise as much as a month or more's worth of purchases value in cash.

3 Can you press your debtors harder for your money? Often regular customers can be brought into your plans and asked to help at a strategically important point by paying considerably earlier than normal. Simply by reducing the number of days credit you allow them (say from 30 to 15 days) and making a big push to get the money in, will also help. These tactics can again gain you up to a month or more's worth of sales in extra cash.

4 Factoring your debtors will raise immediate cash for you. Your bank will be able to suggest a factoring company to contact. The factoring company lends you money against your outstanding invoices (normally 75 per cent of the value) and either helps you collect the debt, at which point you repay the loan, or they collect the debt and give you the balance of the invoice when it is received. There can be, in addition to the interest on the loan, a service charge for handling the debt. This is a very expensive way of finding finance, but it has kept many companies afloat and allowed many others to pursue their expansion plans.

5 Can you reduce stock without damaging your customer service? This applies both to raw materials and to finished goods. Sizeable amounts of cash can be generated in this way at a particular point in time.

6 Do you have any assets that you do not need that you could sell off to generate cash?

7 Is everyone in your staff pulling their weight? You will have to be careful in this area as any expansion will put considerable pressures on existing staff and further complicating this with redundancies may be counterproductive. Maybe you should have a chat with them and attempt to involve them in your plans in order to motivate them.

> A small protective clothing suppliers solved the problem of an increasingly less productive van driver by putting him in charge of transport including the maintenance of their vehicles which were to increase from two to three in the company's expansion. His attitude changed overnight.

Step 3: Approach your professional advisors

You have already involved your accountant, it is now a good time to approach your bank to discuss the project with them and to see how they can help. You will want to discuss what they will need in the way of information and presentation of your facts.

Both your accountant and your bank manager will be able to suggest other sources of finance and who to contact. You will also get good advice and often financial support in the form of interest-free loans for a given period, from the economic development office of your local authority, assuming that they have a policy of helping local businesses. If you have a development agency in your area like the Scottish Development Agency or

Welsh Development Agency, you will find them very helpful and may even be the source of some of your funding requirement. If you are seeking grant aid, such as Regional Selective Assistance, from central government sources, it is essential to involve the regional office of the Department of Trade and Industry, who make these payments, from the outset. Grants will not be paid retrospectively if work has already started on a project.

Step 4: Determine what sources of funding are relevant to you

The following list of broad sources are meant to give you a guide as to what different funders expect in return for their money.

1 Banks. Although banks will get involved in any size of loan, they are not risk takers and will expect you to inject a meaningful percentage sum into the project to show your commitment to the venture. They will also look for any security that is available. It is difficult to be precise as to amounts, but the nearer you are to matching the funds you require with money from other sources, the better your chances of success in negotiating a loan. If your bank won't look at the package then try someone else. However, it is generally accepted that it is the exception rather than the rule that another bank will offer you more money. This is basically because your own bank knows you, and if you have been doing well they will have a much clearer view of your capabilities and will be more confident to lend this extra measure of financial support.

Banks are suppliers nonetheless, and you shouldn't be afraid to negotiate over the interest rate that they want to charge you. This applies equally to bank charges.

> One garden machinery equipment hirer had his banker come round to his office to discuss the terms of a loan he wanted for an extension to his premises. He was particularly pleased when he had beaten his bank manager down to two and a quarter per cent interest above base rate. However, the owner-manager could not resist having a go at trying to reduce this interest rate even further and in subsequent negotiations this was discussed and a lower figure eventually agreed upon.

You can expect to pay anything from one per cent to four per cent above base rate for this sort of money. In general overdrafts will tend to be slightly more expensive than term loans. If security is a problem then the government's Loan Guarantee Scheme is something to explore in that it guarantees up to 70 per cent of the loan (maximum loan £100,000). However, the interest rate is correspondingly higher – usually around one to two per cent above a traditional bank facility.

Remember that you will be expected to provide the bank with a detailed business plan to get the money, and monthly accounts thereafter.

2 Government grants. Many government grants have been covered in previous chapters but fig. 11.1 covers the main ones.

Type of grant	Amount	Restrictions
Enterprise Initiative (help towards the cost of hiring consultants to improve your business)	Half (two-thirds in Assisted Areas) of the cost of between five and fifteen consultancy days	Less than 500 employees Independent company
Regional Investment Grants	Up to £15,000	Less than 25 employees Development Areas only
Regional Innovation Grant	Up to £25,000	50 per cent funding Less than 25 employees Development Areas only
Regional Selective Assistance (help towards getting an expansion plan off the ground)	Minimum necessary for project to go ahead Based on capital expenditure and/or jobs created	Assisted Areas only Manufacturing and service sectors only
Export Market Research (help with market research overseas and can be done by your own staff)	Up to half of cost (up to maximum of £20,000)	
Business Growth Training (help from consultants to assess training needs and train you and your staff for the changes due to expansion)	Half the costs (up to a maximum of £15,000)	Less than 500 employees

Fig. 11.1 Government grants

Grants generally are more widely available if you are in an Assisted Area (generally areas of high unemployment and industrial generation problems), are involved in manufacturing and if you are not owned or controlled by a large company. However, some grants extend throughout the country and are available to all firms, so contact your local office of the DTI in England, Industry Department for Scotland in Scotland and Welsh Industry Department in Wales, or your Local Enterprise Agency for details.

Obviously grant money is free but there are often strings attached, not the least of which are that the money must be used for the purpose designated and that the company be open for visits from time to time by trade and similar delegations. Remember, there is no such thing as an 'automatic' grant, everything is now 'by negotiation', and you must identify a need to gain support.

3 Building societies, insurance companies and merchant banks. If your project involves the acquisition or development of property, insurance companies are increasingly interested in helping. They will normally provide loans at fairly advantageous rates, possibly without repayment during the development phase.

Building societies are nowadays much more interested in lending money and you should certainly talk to your local branch to see if they can help in any way. Again, property is normally the area that they are most interested in. They may provide extra personal funds against the value of your own home.

Merchant banks are keen to get involved in the larger sums of money and often provide funds alongside a venture capitalist. They are particularly keen to help management buyouts. Your bank manager will be able to put you in touch with your bank's merchant banking firm.

4 The Business Expansion Scheme. Individuals who invest in a small company in which they have no vested interest and will not therefore have a controlling share (less than 30 per cent), are entitled to tax relief on their investment at their maximum rate of income tax. They must however, keep their money in for at least five years to retain this tax advantage. Many individuals and customers invest money into a smaller business in order to take full advantage of these tax benefits. Basically they are looking for an increasing annual dividend and a reasonably guaranteed method of exit after five years. Normally this will take the form of some sort of buy-back clause whereby you will have the option to purchase their shares at the end of five years.

The attraction of this scheme is that you don't have to give up control of your business as the individual investor is unlikely to interfere. Equally, the investor does not require security (unlike the banks). However, the BES fund normally appoints someone to the board on a non-executive capacity in an endeavour to closely monitor the situation. Also, in the long run, it can be expensive money as the investor is looking for over ten times his or her investment back after five years.

Details of the BES can be obtained from the DTI or your nearest Local Enterprise Agency.

5 Local authority schemes. Many local authorities are now setting up loan and equity schemes to help small businesses in their area. These schemes are not necessarily well publicized and it is recommended that you contact your local authority to find out what they have on offer. Their terms are normally very advantageous with capital moratoriums and either zero or low interest rates on loans. The equity schemes will often be looking for a much smaller rate of return than the BES investors. They may, however, only support certain industry sectors.

6 British Coal and British Steel funds. With the closure of many pits and steel works throughout Europe, the European Community have set up a loan fund under the auspices of the European Coal and Steel Community (ECSC). This fund will lend from £5000 to £3 million (or more in some cases) although the effective ceiling for small businesses is £500,000. The loans are towards projects that create employment opportunities in coal and steel closure areas (the DTI will provide you with details of where these areas are in Britain). Interest is at attractive rates, although fixed at the outset of the project and a rebate of two or three per cent on the interest may be paid for the first five years depending on the jobs created and the eligibility of former coal and steel workers for them. The loans (for up to 50 per cent of the fixed asset cost of the project) are available to manufacturing and service companies, and the project must involve expenditure on fixed assets and create at least two new jobs. The amount of the loan (which is normally for eight years with a four year moratorium on capital repayments) is roughly calculated at £9000 per job created which is eligible for the interest rebate, plus a further £9000 per job created which is not eligible for the interest rebate. Your bank may be an agent for the fund, so contact them or 3i, who are the national agents. Application can also be made direct to British Coal Enterprises or British Steel (Industry) Ltd who can offer smaller amounts (less than £25,000) on very favourable terms. ECSC funds may be available outside coal and steel closure areas provided the jobs created employ former coal and steel workers.

7 An entrepreneur. There are an increasing number of individuals who are willing to invest, in some cases, large sums of money in your firm but for a large share of the action, for instance, they will normally want to be involved in the running of the firm. Buying them out can be a problem, and if you don't find the right person it could have serious long-term effects on your business and your motivation. Although these people do have a lot of contacts and many of them are genuine, you must be wary of 'gift horses', particularly if you are finding other funding sources difficult. You will normally have to pay for this person's time in your firm unless it is an equity investment and this can be expensive as well as expansive. You will have to accept a lot of help or alternatively hassle from this person so make absolutely sure you feel you have made the right decision before you go down this route. Partners in industry have a fairly chequered history of success. *Venture Capital Report,* a monthly publication of information about companies who are looking for funding and these sorts of sources of finance, is a useful means of finding out about and getting in contact with these people. It can be obtained from:

Venture Capital Report, Boston Rd, Henley-on-Thames RG9 1DY. Tel: 0491 579999.

8 Venture capitalists. When you are looking for sums over £100,000 or in some cases £200,000 the venture capitalists are your best bet. 3i are probably the best known in this area, but your accountant will be able to suggest others.

Venture capitalists are looking for a sizeable return on their investment of upwards of 30 per cent. This is because they will invest in more risky projects, lose money more often and need some means to cover themselves. The exact deal that they will strike with you will depend on the risk involved, your assets and the projected growth of the firm. They will be most interested in how they will ultimately get out of the deal, so you should be considering public floatation or selling off in the future. Or you could negotiate a buy-back arrangement. The venture capitalist will also want a seat on the board and may even seek a controlling interest if he feels that this is necessary considering the finance required and the state of your firm.

9 Funding packages. It is better to try to get a number of different funders together in a package of funding sources rather than to rely too heavily on one source. While you may find that initially only one source is willing to help, you will be amazed at the change of heart many funders have when they find others have already taken the plunge.

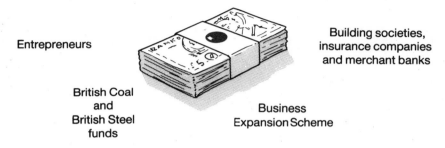

Banks

Venture
capitalists

Government grants

Entrepreneurs

Building societies,
insurance companies
and merchant banks

British Coal
and
British Steel
funds

Business
Expansion Scheme

Local authority
schemes

Fig. 11.2 Sources of finance

Action

1 Calculate roughly how much money you require for your
   expansion plans. In setting up your cash flow try to use a
   computer spreadsheet programme such as Lotus 1-2-3 or
   Supercalc. It will make changes a hundred times easier and
   shorten the time of the whole process dramatically.
2 Approach all the sources of funds in your area for details of
   what they can provide and what they want in terms of plans
   and security and return on their investment.
3 Draw up a business plan, altering it to suit the particular
   funder, and go round all of them, attempting to get their
   commitment to fund you.
4 Decide what you will take from where, bearing in mind:

   a cost
   b control
   c return
   d interference

12 Coping with expansion

Aims of this chapter

- To help you get started with your expansion plans
- To help you find time for your expansion plans
- To give you some tips on influencing others to help you with your expansion plans
- To suggest how you can get the best out of your staff through appropriate leadership
- To explain how you can have effective meetings to further your expansion plans
- To suggest how you can survive the stress of expansion

Now that this book has gone through all the technicalities of successful expansion, this final chapter will look at how you can actually make it happen.

Getting started

This is probably the most difficult part of expansion – not just at the beginning but also at frequent points along the way when perhaps your motivation is low or there are too many problems for you to tackle. The first thing to try is jotting something, anything, down on a notebook or piece of paper. An A4 spiral notebook is useful, but choose something that you yourself find useful (some people like 3″ x 4″ cards that they can keep in their pocket so that they can put down their thoughts as they come to them). The important thing is to get something down on paper.

A technique which is very useful for organizing your thoughts is described by Tony Buzan in his book *Use Your Head*. Start with the area you are working on in the centre of your paper or card and then jot thoughts down, grouping like thoughts together and extending some of these thoughts into various possibilities. By the end of five minutes you will probably have filled the page and it will look a little like a spider's web, with your various chains of thought running out from the centre. Now make a list of things that need to be done, or you need to find out. Create the necessary pressure for you to do something by arranging a meeting at which you will have to have done the things required, or find out the information needed. Sometimes arranging to see a friend or your accountant to discuss your plans can be sufficient incentive to ensure you don't turn up without having done some homework.

You may find keeping all your thoughts and plans in your diary is more your way of doing things and certainly the time management or *filofax* type diaries can be very useful. Alternatively, you may like to keep a loose-leaf folder and put into it any information, articles, notes, meeting agendas, and so on. The main thing is to get started now – today! Waiting for next week or when you are less busy or after the next project will mean that you will wait for ever.

Finding the time

Most small business people are extremely busy and if your business is growing at the moment, you will know how the day to day pressures make it extremely difficult to find the time to actively do anything about your expansion plans. So, the first thing to do is:

Make time to make time

You need to find a few minutes to sit down quietly to plan how you are going to find more time. Useful periods of thinking time include:

a when you are driving
b when you are waiting to see someone in their offices
c when you are on holiday
d on a Sunday afternoon
e by getting up an hour earlier once a week
f while you are having a bath or a shower
g whenever you find you have a few minutes to yourself

Your first thought has to be when can you arrange half an hour or thereabouts every week to plan out what you are going to do in the next week? This is your 'personal coaching and tactics' meeting. On a page of your notebook or diary, list all the things that you need to do in the coming week. Now add some things that you need to do for your expansion plan. Decide the priorities of these things and where possible to whom you will delegate them. By this simple action, the half hour spent each week will free up anything from a few hours to a day or two of time to concentrate on your expansion plans.

Each day make a list of things to do that day and prioritize them. Ask yourself: 'does this really need to be done' and if the answer is yes, 'does it really need to be done by me?' Once you have completed a task or delegated it, cross it off or tick it. This way, at the end of the day, you can see that you have got some things done, even although all of your list may not have been completed. If you do delegate a task, make sure that you make a note of the task and who you delegated it to in your diary so that you can check up on it later.

Having a 'page a day' diary is essential for efficient working. By noting down your future actions as well as meetings into your diary, you can forget about having to remember to do things. They are there for you to do on the appropriate day. This saves a lot of time spent trying to remember what you had to do. As will be seen later, further time can also be saved by making your meetings more efficient and by delegating more effectively.

Winning people over to your way of thinking

Be it selling, or negotiating with your bank manager, or motivating your staff, you are always having to win people over to your way of thinking. Still the best book on this subject is Dale Carnegie's *How to Win Friends and Influence People*. Even if you have to wrap it in brown paper so that your friends don't know you are consulting it, you should still read it as it is an essential work of reference for the task ahead.

Here are a few thoughts on how to get people round to your way of thinking:

1 Start by being friendly. Try to win the person over as your friend or at least show him or her that you are interested in, and care about, them. Listening intently is a good starting point.

2 Get the other person to do most of the talking. People often say, 'he's a good salesman' when they mean 'he's a good talker'. The really good salesperson is the one that helps and influences you to buy without you even realizing it. Ask open ended questions that don't elicit a straight yes or no answer.

3 Ask why. Try to delve behind people's surface answers or opinions to get at their real reasons or thoughts.

4 Try to see things from the other person's point of view. How would you feel or react if you were in their shoes? How can you use this understanding to help you handle the situation better?

5 Try to get them to think the solution is their idea. By asking people for their thoughts on how to solve a problem you have with them, you can sometimes get them to come up with solutions that will suit you.

6 Don't dismiss the other person's view. The quickest way to put barriers up between you and someone else is to say, 'that won't work' or 'that's a stupid idea' or 'your wrong', even if they are. Try saying 'that's fascinating' instead and see how quickly this will change their view of you.

7 Reward frequently. Even the slightest movement towards your point of view should be rewarded. Reward can be simply smiling or nodding your head to saying 'great' or 'I agree'.

8 Think through your interaction before you make it. Try to visualize for a moment or two before you interact with someone, how you want the meeting or conversation to go. Think of all the benefits for the other person of agreeing with you and 'see' them coming round to your point of view with enthusiasm. It won't work out every time as you may have imagined but it does get you thinking of the positives that will move the person rather than the negatives.

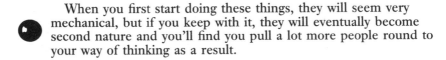

When you first start doing these things, they will seem very mechanical, but if you keep with it, they will eventually become second nature and you'll find you pull a lot more people round to your way of thinking as a result.

Leadership and motivation

If you are going to succeed with your expansion plans, you will need to provide leadership that motivates those around you. What a lot of small business owners fail to grasp is that different people need different styles of leadership. Basically it depends on the person's level of competence and motivation.

1 High competence, high motivation. These are your 'best' people. Here you simply have to delegate the whole task to them and let them get on with it. Make sure that you:

 a establish the person's work priorities
 b give clear instructions concerning the task to be carried out and the measurement for success
 c give the appropriate power to the person carrying out the job and make sure that they are accountable for the result
 d make a regular assessment of the person's skills experience and motivation to make sure it is appropriate to delegate a particular task to them
 e make time and provide opportunities for periods of consultation and suggestion making

2 High competence, low motivation. Good people that have gone off the boil. You need to spend time re-coaching these people. Identify the problems and try jointly to solve them. Keep building the person up and don't go for any length of time without seeing them. Reward frequently and treat as equal with compassion but firmness.

3 Low competence, high motivation. Generally the young, new recruits in your organization. These people need training and either this training should come from you or be organized by you. Their motivation will not be dampened if you can ensure that they don't fail too often. Make tasks simple but stretching and recap what has been learnt all the time. You, or someone else, will have to spend a lot of time with these people when they tackle a new task, but they are motivating to be with because they are so keen.

4 Low competence, low motivation. Your potential 'deadwood'. Highly directional leadership is required here: 'please do this and then do that'. The mere fact that activity is generated may increase motivation and you can then move on to training. Don't be afraid to be firm and heavily directional with this group if you want to achieve something from them. Your attention may help raise their motivation.

Using the wrong style of leadership can be disastrous. For example, heavily directional leadership with a highly motivated and competent person can quickly lead to them being dissatisfied and demotivated and eventually leaving.

Trying to motivate people is hard but here are a few pointers:

a set attainable but stretching targets
b make the person believe they can be successful by telling them so
c negotiate targets with the person concerned and agree ones that you *and* they feel they can achieve
d celebrate the successful achievement of the target by also telling the person's peer group and by openly congratulating them

Having effective meetings

As your organization grows, so do the number of meetings. Many business owners would like to, and sometimes do, do away with meetings all together. However, meetings are important for communication, generating ideas, getting commitment, building motivation, and making decisions that people will carry through. So, how can you cut down on the number of them and shorten the time taken by each of them?

1 Why? First ask yourself: what is the purpose of this meeting? Then review if a meeting is the best way to achieve the purpose. This helps you clarify the aim of the meeting and, therefore, who should attend.

2 Who? The second question is: who should attend? Is everybody necessary and if necessary, do they need to be at the whole meeting? There is nothing more irritating or demotivating than to have to sit through a meeting in which there are large portions that are irrelevant to you and you are irrelevant to the discussion and outcome.

3 Where? Where is the most appropriate place to have the meeting? If there are just two of you and you want to control the time it takes then it may be easier for you to visit them, then you can leave whenever you want to. Sometimes meeting in the corridor will keep the conversation short. For larger groups, make sure the room is comfortable and well ventilated – you don't want your employees dropping off! Also make sure you won't be interrupted – take the 'phone off the hook or tell your secretary to take messages.

4 When? When should the meeting take place? Make sure the time is appropriate for all those attending. Sometimes, if you want action, arranging a meeting with a particular person for a few minutes after you have spoken on the 'phone can have the psychological impact of importance, particularly if you offer to go to them. One major point: **always** start on time.

5 What? What will you discuss? Every meeting should have an agenda, even if it is just between you and someone else. If there are several people then agree a timetable for each item and stick to it. Another meeting can always be arranged for issues that come up and sticking to an agenda really helps focus the mind on getting the work of the meeting done.

6 How? How will you achieve the objectives of the meeting? First of all make sure that everyone is clear what the objectives of the meeting are. Try to involve everyone in discussions and open up discussion to the whole group before going for specific people's viewpoints. Agree how you will make decisions and don't leave an agenda item without first clarifying the decisions made and actions required. Keep to the timing of the meeting. Be firm but attentive to all views and opinions.

7 Then? After the meeting, what happens then? Make sure you produce a one page minute within 24 hours of the meeting. Long minutes are a waste of everybody's time and don't get read. The minute should have a column down the right hand side headed 'Action' and the people responsible for carrying out the actions referred to in the minute should have their initials in this column next to the appropriate action. Use the appropriate leadership style to follow up (if necessary) the action points of the meeting to ensure that progress is made. If you involve people in the process of making the decisions or agreeing the actions, then you are much more likely to see them carried out.

No growth occurs without strain

Most people involved in business enjoy it because of the cut and thrust and the pressure it puts them under to perform and achieve. However, too much pressure for too long can lead to stress and this can lead to all manner of health disorders and loss of effectiveness. So before you embark on even more pressure by expanding your business, make sure your family or partner is behind you. You may find this your biggest and most difficult 'selling' job. However don't side step it because you will need their support and encouragement when the going gets tough. Remember how to influence people to your way of thinking. Just because they are close to you doesn't mean to say that they don't need persuading or enthusing.

Once you have your domestic support, start building support within your firm. You will need someone you can turn to for help and understanding. This is often your secretary or assistant. You need someone to 'look after' you. Don't forget to show your appreciation by keeping them informed of what you are doing, what your mission statement is and means, and by showing that you care about them and their problems as well.

However, even if you gain all this support, things can still get out of hand. There are three important things to do:

1 **Learn to relax.** This doesn't mean going home and just watching the television but means actually physically relaxing. Yoga or meditation may help or just a good long soak in a hot bath – but you have got to learn how and do it frequently. At work, simply counting your breaths for one minute, then doing it again but this time trying to take less breaths, will help you to relax. You must take time off – both at weekends and for holidays. Not only does it make you more effective it also gives you time to think creatively and plan ahead.

2 **Get some exercise.** Exercise keeps you fit and healthy and also makes you more alert. If you find yourself yawning a lot, try going for a brisk walk for half an hour each day and you'll find that the yawning will disappear. It also gives you time to think and plan.

3 **Get in control.** The greatest source of stress is when you don't feel in control. If you can't pay your bills, or can't get anyone to help you with your expansion plans then stress begins to set in. The only thing to do is to try to get back into control. Split the

problem into smaller and more manageable bits. Ask the help of friends or advisors (a problem shared is a problem often more than halved). Set up a 'think tank' within your company.

When one owner of a small advertising agency found that he could not pay the bills he eventually 'phoned all the creditors and made arrangements to pay them in instalments, sometimes over several months. Now that he was in control he was able to think clearly and started to use the same method to get the debtors to pay him more regularly. He got many of them on a standing order and soon found that what had seemed like an insoluble situation with people shouting at him from all directions, became the basis for a successful business and a useful strategy for further expansion.

Action

Go for it!

Expanding your business is like seeing a child grow up. It is at once exciting, inspiring, frightening, depressing, exhilarating, but ultimately immensely satisfying. If you want your business to grow – go for it and make it happen. Good luck!

Appendix A

Suggested further reading

The following books are those that you might find useful or motivational on particular and general subjects.

A Passion for Excellence, T. Peters and N. Austen, Fontana.

An Insight into Management Accounting, J. Sizer, Pelican.

Don't Do. Delegate! J. M. Jenks and J. M. Kelly, Kogan Page.

Everything is Negotiable, How to Negotiate and Win, G. Kennedy, Arrow.

Further Up the Organization, R. Townsend, Harper & Row.

Getting to Yes, Negotiating Agreement Without Giving In, R. Fisher and W. Ury, Business Books.

Going for Growth, A Guide to Corporate Strategy, M. K. Lawson, Kogan Page.

How to Win Friends and Influence People, D. Carnegie, Pocket Books.

Innovation: The Attacker's Advantage, R. Foster, Pan.

Leadership and the One Minute Manager, K. Blanchard, P. Zigarmi and D. Zigarmi, Fontana.

Making It Happen, J. Harvey-Jones, Collins.

Managing for Results, P. Drucker, Pan.

Managing Your Company's Finances, R. L. Hargreaves and R. H. Smith, Heinemann.

Opportunities, E. de Bono, Penguin.

Raising Finance, The Guardian Guide for the Small Business, C. Woodcock, Kogan Page.

Successful Marketing for the Small Business, D. Patten, Kogan Page.

Taking up a Franchise, G. Goben and C. Barrow, Kogan Page.

The Creative Gap: Managing Ideas for Profit, S. Major, Longman.

The Generation of Ideas for New Products, T. Sowery, Kogan Page.

The Genghis Khan Guide to Business, B. Warnes, Osmosis Publications.

The Magic of Thinking Big, D. J. Schwartz, Cornerstone Library.

The New Small Business Guide, Sources of Information for New and Small Businesses, C. Barrow, BBC Publications.

The One Minute Manager, K. Blanchard and S. Johnson, Collins Willow.

The Practice of Management, P. Drucker, Pan.

Use Your Head, T. Buzan, BBC Books.

What They Don't Teach You at Harvard Business School, M. McCormack, Collins.

In addition most of the large accountancy firms, banks and 3i have useful booklets on many of the topics discussed in this book.

Appendix B

Useful addresses

Association of British Chambers of Commerce, Sovereign House, 212a Shaftesbury Ave, London WC2H 8EW. Tel: 01-240 5831/6.

British Coal Enterprises (for grant and loan information for expansion in coal closure areas):
Scotland Tel: 0259 218021, *Western* Tel: 0942 672404, *South Wales* Tel: 0222 761671, *South East* Tel: 0227 61477, *North East* Tel: 091-487 8822, *Yorkshire* Tel: 0302 727228, *Midlands* Tel: 0623 554747.

British Direct Marketing Association, Grosvenor Gardens House, 35 Grosvenor Gdns, London SW1W 0BS. Tel: 01-242 2254.

British Franchise Association, 75a Bell St, Henley-on-Thames RG9 2BD. Tel: 0491 578049/50.

British Institute of Management, Operations Centre, Management House, Cottingham Rd, Corby NN17 1TT. Tel: 0536 204222.

British Overseas Trade Board, 1-19 Victoria St, London SW1H 0ET. Tel: 01-215 7877.

British Steel (Industry) Ltd (for grant and loan information for expansion in steel closure areas):
Canterbury House, 2-6 Sydenham Rd, Croyden CR9 2LJ. Tel: 01-686 2311.

British Venture Capital Association, 1 Surrey St, London WC2R 2PS. Tel: 01-836 5702.

Business in the Community, 227a City Rd, London EC1 4GH. Tel: 01-253 3716.

Confederation of British Industry (CBI), Centre Point, 103 New Oxford St, London WC1A 1DU. Tel: 01-379 7400.

Department of Trade and Industry (for details of grant, loan and other assistance to business in your area):
DTI North East: Stanegate House, 2 Groat Market, Newcastle upon Tyne NE1 1YN. Tel: 091-235 7292.
DTI North West (Liverpool): Graeme House, Derby Sq, Liverpool L2 7UP. Tel: 051-224 6300.
DTI North West (Manchester): 75 Mosley St, Manchester M2 3HR. Tel: 061-838 5000.
DTI Yorkshire and Humberside: 4th Floor, Fairfax House, Merrion St, Leeds LS2 8JU. Tel: 0532 338300.
DTI Midlands: Severns House, 20 Middle Pavement, Nottingham NG1 7DW. Tel: 0602 596460.
DTI West Midlands: Ladywood House, Stephenson St, Birmingham B2 4DT. Tel: 021-631 6181.
DTI South East: Ebury Bridge House, 2-18 Ebury Bridge Rd, London SW1W 8QD. Tel: 01-730 8451.

DTI South West: The Pithay, Bristol BS1 2PBN. Tel: 0272 308400.
Scotland: Industry Department for Scotland, Alhambra House, 45 Waterloo St, Glasgow G2 6AT. Tel: 041-248 2855.

Franchise Development Services, Castle House, Castle Meadow, Norwich NR2 1PJ. Tel: 0603 620301.

Highlands and Islands Development Board: Bridge House, 27 Bank St, Inverness IV1 1QR. Tel: 0463 234171.

Institute of Personnel Management (IPM), IPM House, 35 Camp Rd, London SW19 4UX. Tel: 01-946 9100.

The Institute of International Licensing Practitioners Ltd, Suite 78, Kent House, 87 Regent St, London W1R 7HF. Tel: 01-439 7091.

3i (Investors in Industry), 91 Waterloo Rd, London SE1 8XP. Tel: 01-928 7822.

Scottish Development Agency, 21 Bothwell St, Glasgow G2 6NR. Tel: 041-248 7806/7.

Small Firms Centres (provided by the Department of Employment to help owner-managers of small firms with their plans and problems):
Birmingham: 9th Floor, Alpha Tower, Suffolk St, Queensway, Birmingham B1 1TT. Tel: 021-643 3844.
Bristol: 6th Floor, The Pithay, Bristol BS1 2PBN. Tel 0272 294546.
Cambridge: Carlyle House, Carlyle Rd, Cambridge CB4 3DN. Tel: 0223 63312.
Cardiff: 16 St David's House, Wood St, Cardiff CF1 1ER. Tel: 0222 396116.
Glasgow: 120 Bothwell St, Glasgow G2 6NR. Tel: 041-248 6014.
Leeds: 1 Park Row, City Sq, Leeds LS1 5NR. Tel: 0532 44515.
Liverpool: Graeme House, Derby Sq, Liverpool L2 7UP. Tel: 051-236 5756.
London: Ebury Bridge House, 18 Ebury Bridge Rd, London SW1W 8QD. Tel: 01-730 8451.
Manchester: 26/28 Deansgate, Manchester M3 1RH. Tel: 061-832 5282.
Newcastle: 15th Floor, Cale Cross House, 156 Pilgrim St, Newcastle upon Tyne NE1 6PZ. Tel: 091-232 5353.
Nottingham: Severns House, 20 Middle Pavement, Nottingham NG1 7DW. Tel: 0602 481184.
Reading: Abbey Hall, Abbey Sq, Reading RG1 3BE. Tel: 0734 591733.
Stevenage: Business and Technology Centre, Bessemer Drive, Stevenage SG1 2DX. Tel: 0438 743377.

The Chartered Institute of Marketing, Moor Hall, Cookham, Maidenhead SL6 9QH. Tel: 06285 24933.

The Industrial Society, Robert Hyde House, 48 Bryanston Sq, London W1H 7LN. Tel: 01-262 2401.

The Training Agency, Moorfoot, Sheffield S1 4PQ. Tel: 0742 703570.

Venture Capital Report, Boston Rd, Henley-on-Thames RG9 1DY. Tel: 0491 579999.

Welsh Development Agency, Business Development Centre, Treforest Industrial Estate, Pontypridd CF37 5UT. Tel: 0443 841777.

Index